AF822987

Information Technology and Law

Information Technology and Law

Edited by
Wojciech Cyrul

Jagiellonian University Press

Reviewer
prof. dr hab. Bartosz Brożek

Cover design
Pracownia Register

The publication of this volume was financed by the National Science Centre

© Copyright by Wojciech Cyrul & Jagiellonian University Press
First edition, Kraków 2014
All rights reserved

No part of this book may be reprinted or reproduced or utilized in any form or by any electronic, mechanical or other means, now know or hereafter invented, including photocopying and recording, or in any information storage or retrieval system, without permission in writing from the publishers.

ISBN 978-83-233-3658-7

WYDAWNICTWO
UNIWERSYTETU
JAGIELLOŃSKIEGO

www.wuj.pl

Jagiellonian University Press
Editorial Offices: Michałowskiego St. 9/2, 31-126 Kraków
Phone: +48 12 663 23 81, +48 12 663 23 82, Fax: +48 12 663 23 83
Distribution: Phone: +48 12 631 01 97, Fax: +48 12 631 01 98
Cell Phone: +48 506 006 674, e-mail: sprzedaz@wuj.pl
Bank: PEKAO SA, IBAN PL80 1240 4722 1111 0000 4856 3325

Contents

Preface

The computerization of legal turnover, legal drafting and the application of law is gradually making them dependent on information technology. This justifies the importance of a number of considerations concerning the technological dimension of legal practice. Given the potential benefits and risks associated with the progressive digitalization and computerization of legislation and the growing importance of the Internet, the issue of the role and uses of information systems in the legal domain requires careful, multi-dimensional analysis.

The impact of information technology on law is still an open question. However, there is no doubt that these technologies are changing the way in which law is created, communicated, applied and interpreted, since they provide new ways of sharing, searching, communicating and analyzing legal information. Communication imposes on human practices and, in particular on legal practices, many specific requirements and restrictions. Therefore, the implementation of new technologies into communication processes can not only help to overcome some traditional problems, such as allowing, for instance, the improvement of existing practices, but it may also cause new problems or make old ones even graver. For example, the development of information technologies may result in the creation of new goods and services, or may change the scope or the field of application of traditional ones. It makes new risks appear, requiring the reinterpretation of existing rules or the introduction of new regulations. However, the need for the reinterpretation of existing law infringes upon its certainty and the introduction of new regulations is costly and complicated. Moreover, inaccurate regulation may have far reaching consequences both for legal systems and existing or future social practices. Thus, one can argue that law, information technologies and social practices are increasingly mutually dependent. Therefore, understanding the causes, trends and significance of the changes resulting from the implementation of information technology in processes related to the creation and application of law is only possible through interdisciplinary research conducted jointly by representatives of various sciences, in particular by computer scientists and lawyers.

This book constitutes the result of a project, whose aim was to bring together computer scientists, legal theoreticians and practitioners and to reflect jointly on how information technologies can be used in legal practice and what changes they may bring to it. The book consists of 9 chapters which analyze various aspects of the computerization of law and the legal problems resulting from developments in IT.

In Chapter 1 Jacek Janowski analyses, how information technology and the Internet in particular can influence law and its axiology. On this basis, he claims that technological development is responsible for the destabilization of law, questioning various positions including classical legal positivism. As a result, a new global and network-related legal culture is developing, called Internet legal culture.

In Chapter 2 Janusz Opila and Tomasz Pełech-Pilichowski outline the basic problems of the storage and presentation of information in the context of coding of the meaning of words and signs. They also discuss selected problems connected with the permanent preservation of data and information stating its relevance for legal text processing. Due to this discussion they claim that the storage and presentation of information is a problem of the digitalization of meaning.

In Chapter 3 Jerzy Duda discusses XML models for legal documents, focusing on the problem of development of a single national XML standard for legal purposes and its compatibility with transnational standards. He presents basic concepts related to the application of XML language in the legal domain and selected examples of XML Schemas for national and transnational legal systems. On this basis, he outlines the development of XML legal standard in Poland and analyses its compatibility with transnational standards.

Chapter 4 presents new possibilities for the similarity analysis of legal documents. Piotr Potiopa compares various methods of the semantic analysis of legal texts, showing, how they can improve the quality of information provided by lawyers. Based on a presentation of selected methods used in text similarity analysis, he shows that analysis of legal documents using semantic relations of lexical units existing in WordNet gives better results than those where semantic relations are not taken into account.

Chapter 5 addresses the issue of changes in the consolidation of legal information resulting from digitalization of legal documents. It outlines how on-line promulgation changes legislative practices related to the management of legal documents. In particular, the problem of the automation of the consolidation of electronic legal documents is presented. On this basis, Wojciech Cyrul analyses the question of whether the more frequent promulgation of authentic consolidated versions of legal texts is able to deal with the reduced clarity of legal texts which results from their numerous and extensive novelizations.

In Chapter 6 Fryderyk Zoll analyses the potential impact of the hyperlinking of different parts of a code on the pandectistic structure of legal texts. He argues that new technology enables a new form of presenting legal texts, facilitating their usage. Based on the example of the Acquis Principles he presents the concept of "mirror structure" and argues that the Acquis Principles may prove their full functionality only if displayed in three dimensions.

Chapter 7 explores the impact of information technology and social media on the channels of participation and democracy in the Swedish model of labour law, where the social partners are in essence given a law-making function through collective agreements. Laura Carlson describes the Swedish labour law model, then the relationship between the social partners and their members. The use of information technology and social media is then described, with the conclusion addressing the issue of whether this use exacerbates the distinction between the insiders and outsiders of the model, enhancing or restricting democracy in the work place.

Chapter 8 discusses the legal status of consumers in digital content contracts concluded over the Internet in EU law. It presents legal problems resulting from the development of e-commerce and the appearance of new types of goods and new ways of selling products and services. Agnieszka Kubiak-Cyrul outlines current EU regulations concerning consumer protection and presents the difficulties in this area resulting from the lack of regulation which recognises the particular nature of digital content.

Finally, in Chapter 9, Lorenz Schulz discusses the impact that the acceleration resulting from digitalisation may have in criminal law. Based on legal and philosophical investigations he argues that this acceleration especially influences the concept of imputation in substantial criminal law and claims that, in criminal trials, acceleration can lead to the infringement of the rights of the suspect in favour of the economy of prosecution.

Chapter 1

Technological Destabilization of Law

Jacek Janowski
Maria Curie-Skłodowska University

1. Introduction

Nowadays, many publications are being written about the information culture which is the system of attitudes to the information and communication technologies.[1] It constitutes an aspect of the development of an information society, conditioned to a degree by the intellectual liberation from the forces and resources of the nature. It is a kind of culture, based on a state of knowledge and the forms of social coexistence, using the information technologies. Its specific area is a culture of the Internet. According to Castells, this culture of the Internet is composed of four freedom cultures: the techno-meritocratic (technical), the hacker (creative), the communitarian (communal) and the managerial (entrepreneurial) cultures.[2]

The nature of the Internet is shaped not only by Internet surfers such as Internet technocrats, hackers, communitarians and managers, but also by the legislator. We can speak about its genetic and internal self-regulation and about the subsequent and external state regulation. The increasing impor-

[1] Compare: W. Furmanek, *Kultura techniczna i kultura informacyjna* (Technical culture and information culture), Kraków 2002.

[2] M. Castells, *Galaktyka Internetu: refleksje nad Internetem, biznesem i społeczeństwem* (The Internet Galaxy: Reflections on the Internet, Business and Society), translated by T. Hornowski, Poznań 2003, p. 48. According to M. Castells, today the most essential processes organize themselves around the networks creating the new social morphology, and it can be added, the new "anatomy of law". For the diffusion and convergency of the network solutions changes the perception and understanding of the phenomena, events and relations in significant degree.

tance of the Internet is at the same time the cause and the effect of the growing litigiousness of the relations established by it, and the positivisation of the rules worked out within it. We can observe a growing diversification of endogenic and exogenic regulations regarding the Internet, in the direction extending its autonomy, but also its dependence on the State. It is connected with the interpenetration of many spheres – natural and artificial, real and virtual, humanistic and technical.

We may say that the influence of new technologies concentrated around the Internet upon law is total and permanent. Therefore, the phenomenon of the web has versatile and uninterrupted influence on the condition of social relations and the way of the social organization. Once underway, the phenomenon of networking will be intensified, diffused and modified by its architecture throughout successive areas of human (material and spiritual, private and public) activity.

In the existing literature we can read that the development of the Internet undermines the principal assumptions of legal positivism, highlighting its insufficiency when it comes to the explanation of new legal phenomena. This, however, does not mean that the democracy and sovereignty principles are anachronistic, but argue for the need to materialize them more fully in new conditions of the continuous technological revolution and growing cultural revolution.[3] The Information Revolution, also known as the electronic, microelectronic, microprocessor, computer, digital, telematic or teleinformatic revolution, has led to the electronization of the economy, administration, politics and law. The phenomenon of the electronization of law consists in substituting traditional legal relations with electronic relations. It starts with adopting regulations concerning electronic signatures in the subsequent legal systems.[4] However, to a great extent, it only takes place in the phase of the advanced development of the information society, also described as the e-society. Most often unilaterally, it is thought that it comes into being *along with the technicization, informatization and networking of the activities and lives of citizens, organizations and institutions.*[5]

At present, the Internet is a medium of communication, a channel of data transmission, a method of goods distribution, an intermediary in making

---

[3] Compare: W. Pawlett, J. Baudrillard, *Against Banality*, London–New York 2007, p. 84.

[4] The first Act on the electronic signatures in the world was passed on May 9, 1995 in the American state of Utah (The Utah Digital Signature Act), and then they appeared in other states of the USA: California, Florida and others. In Poland, the Act on electronic signatures was passed on September 18, 2001 (Journal of Laws, No. 130, item 1450, as later amended).

[5] L.W. Zacher, *Elektronizacja polityki w społeczeństwie informacyjnym (e-administracja, e-rząd, e-demokracja)* (Electronization of politics in the information society (e-administration, e-government, e-democratization)), in: A. Szewczyk (ed.), *Problemy społeczeństwa informacyjnego* (Problems of the information society), Vol. 1, Szczecin 2007, p. 302.

payments, a tool for socio-technical interaction and coordination of undertakings, an environment for knowledge organization, a support for outsourcing virtual information, a field of information management, and recently also an official teleinformatic publication, a platform for providing public services and a vehicle for promulgation of legal acts. However, taking into account the fact that the Internet is not a closed and self-contained medium, when used it impacts upon real social relations and formal legal statuses. The forming of legal culture in the Internet opposes the hindering of freedom and interference of the state, leading to deregulation and releasing self-regulation in international relations.[6] However, the accumulation of hazards and divergences in the domestic relations forces to the new regulation, and even leads to hyper-regulation.

2. Axiology of technology

The computer is not only a self-learning and self-reproducing technical fact, but it has also started to function as a cultural, social and legal fact. It underwent ideologization, because it was considered to be the so called defining technology.[7] Because it determines different roles and new places for humans in society, the state and the world. It is a kind of advanced technology which, when applied, results in new patterns in the functioning of humans. Such patterns include the handling of tools, simulating phenomena, playing games, executing programs, or reconstructing models.

The starting point in the development of computer law was the statement that the computer is not only a technical tool (as a calculating machine), but also a cultural fact (as a medium of communication) and, in consequence, an object of standardization (as an element of obligation). It constitutes the physical (electromagnetic) realization of a logical model (the Turing machine scheme) of automated (programmable) calculations (mathematical operations). As a technical tool, it is a data processing system (machine) together with an input-output peripheral devices (system). Due to its highly advanced and sophisticated applications, it is not indifferent to legal theory, practice and dogma.

---

[6] According to L. Morawski, transformation from the modernist model of employers and engineers of society to the post-modernist model of interpreters and mediators is the answer to the transformation of the world that surrounds us. The same: *What postmodernism can give to the learning of law*, Toruń 2001, p. 43.

[7] Compare: W.J. Bober, *Powinność w świecie cyfrowym: etyka komputerowa w świetle współczesnej filozofii moralnej* (Obligation in the digital world: computer-related ethics in the light of the contemporary moral philosophy), Warszawa 2008, p. 46.

The computer and information technology is subject to the same limitations as technology as a whole. Under the influence of the unexpected consequences of the technical development at the end of the 19th century, an accompanying philosophy developed.[8] This refers to both the action and its products but the technology is a method and a process for the fabrication of something from matter (raw materials) and energy (fuels).[9] Utilization consists in using tools that are, in themselves, axiologically indifferent, as they do not set targets which are external to the technology as a medium.

Wojciech Bober writes, that:

> Making decisions connected with the application of technique takes the form of the instrumental reasoning, in which a person who makes decisions attributes the means to the pre-assumed targets, according to the criteria of their effectiveness (suitability, economics, etc.), i.e., the utilitarian criteria, in accordance with his professional knowledge. As different targets could be achieved using the same means and different means may lead to the same target, the element of decision and selection (assessment) is important here.[10]

And this is subject to evaluation, as with any other human choice, according moral and legal aspects. Axiological neutrality relates, therefore, to the technology as a product, but not as a way of acting.

We have to be aware that:

> Development status of the technical information converters and carriers has enormous influence on the science, culture, economy, environment, social awareness, that is, on the status of development of a particular country and its security. The greater dependence on the technical sphere of information, the greater sensitivity to any potential disturbances and hazards, that have different origins and forms. Therefore, at the root of the global information systems lies the inherent ability to become the dangerous tool, the tool paralysing the world, the instrument of asymmetric struggles and hazards.[11]

It has been stressed that, thanks to cybernetic tools, a single human can declare war on mankind and win. Throughout the entirety of the history of

---

[8] Ibid., p. 17.

[9] A. Rothert writes that the technique is the means (tools), ways (methods) and actions (activities) utilized to make something. As such, it becomes the *key element of the technology understood widely in terms of the system*. A. Rothert, *Cybernetic political order*, Warszawa 2005, p. 22. From the point of view of the matters discussed here, the question posed by the author is interesting – *Can technology constitute an individual environment in which we are closed and undergo transformation?* Ibid., p. 22. A positive answer would explain many of the technical problems of the social acting of law.

[10] W.J. Bober, *Powinność w świecie cyfrowym...* (Obligation in the digital world...), p. 19.

[11] B. Służalska, J. Służalski, *Zagrożenie asymetryczne a społeczeństwo informacyjne* (Asymmetrical hazards and the information society), in: A. Szewczyk (ed.), *Problemy społeczeństwa informacyjnego...* (Problems of the information society...), p. 129.

mankind, people have not managed to develop even a fraction of the dangers and hazards that we hold in the present. This means that technology generates hazards in itself and forces the creation of laws to protect the individual, society and mankind against them.

The hardware and software configuration of the network infrastructure, and the architecture of cybernetic areas, virtual environments, multimedia objects and the digital tools built upon them, leads to ambivalent actions, expressing themselves in the independence and control, autonomy and centralization, anonymity and identification, confidentiality and openness, freedom and restrictions, non-intervention and control. It has been observed that conventional techniques of handling information were characterized by ineffectiveness and inefficiency.[12] This, however, protected the individual against the omnipotence of administration, political domination, economical exploitation and cultural unification. Yet, the popularization of non-conventional techniques of handling the information or the digital, automated and remote processing of data creates substantial changes to that situation. As a result, the range of information resources and the sophistication of information operations has grown radically and has led to the creation of, amongst others, models of behaviour, profiles of personality, parameters of manipulation, simulators of processes, correlators of facts or analyzers connections.

3. Technologization of law

Visions of the information society are most often built on the basis of the technological concepts of the society, and not on the social concepts of technology.[13] This means an interpretation of law in the spirit of the technological and materialistic determinism. The method of avoiding the technologization of the social order and, as a result, the law as the regulator, is the classical and philosophical perception of law itself. Law, understood in the positivist

[12] Ibid., p. 72.

[13] Law and management in the information society refers to two visions of the information society: the humanistic in Europe, where hazards and the need to minimize them are being emphasized, and the technical in North America, emphasizing technological optimism, where more often information infrastructure and data highways are discussed. A. Szewc, *Szanse i zagrożenia w społeczeństwie informacyjnym* (Opportunities and hazards in the information society), in: A. Szewczyk (ed.), *Problemy społeczeństwa informacyjnego...* (Problems of the information society...), p. 133–134. Technology is accepted as the basis for diverse divisions in the societies, including e.g., division into the pre-industrial, industrial or post-industrial societies, according to D. Bell, *The Coming of Post-Industrial Society: A Venture in Social Forecasting*, New York 1999.

sense, is endangered most by the dictators of technology with the pressure of technical possibilities in order to realize social engineering). From the point of view of legal positivism, it is justified to apply any technical means which bring us closer to the political targets outlined.[14] Virtualization and cybernetization creates the perspective to form worlds that are possible and consistent, and also impossible worlds that are internally inconsistent.

The rejection of the interpretation of law in the light of technological determinism is possible in the conditions of the affirmation of the natural order. The technological experiments performed in the name of the information revolution, uncontrolled and unverified on the basis of the classically understood values of truth and good, have caused irreversible social changes and stopped the historical continuity of several processes. From the point of view of philosophically and culturally oriented anthropology of law, they have radically deepened the rift between the nature and the culture being built on top of it. It is easier to describe the external impact of technology on the society, and more difficult to discern the internal social determinants of the development of technology. This is why more attention is being focused on informatization, as the implementation of information technology into the special, political and legal practice, and less on the more basic issues – the social, political and legal determinants of the development of the information technology.

From the point of view of information law, the influence of law on the development of information engineering is being studied and, on the basis of legal data processing, the impact of information engineering on law analysed. However, it is not possible to learn about either of these processes separately: it must be considered as a mutually connected phenomenon. In any reciprocal interaction, one is the first as a cause while the other occurs as the effect, escalating its cause and itself at the same time. But settlement of the eternal dilemma of priority ultimately depends on primary world-philosophical-religious attitudes.

In social life, having a different course in the virtual space than in real space, the law acts.

> The Internet demonstrates the qualitative, and not only the quantitative differences in comparison with the other technically advanced information exchange systems. The most important of them is the global, immediate and permanent accessibility of information, non-territoriality and very difficult control of the data flow.[15]

---

[14] According to L. Morawski; "In the modernistic vision of the society, science [...] becomes the primary production force, law – main instrument to reform the world and scientists – the experts, who show how to realize different visions of the world and the society". L. Morawski, *Co może dać nauce...* (What can be given to science...), p. 28.

[15] K. Dobrzeniecki, *Lex Informatica*, Toruń 2008, p. 10.

These, and other properties of the web discussed in the literature, project on the freedom and reliability of access to information about law (the status of law) and the exchange of information within law (in legal relations). However, freedom and security are the values that underlie the creative activeness of individuals and the cultural products of societies. On the non-territorial, non-temporal and nonmaterial plane of the integrated imagination, a dynamic electronic economy is being built, the most widely accessible electronic democracy, and the fastest legal relations appear.

The unprecedented scale of the data processing phenomena, and the unimaginable perspective of their interaction has caused a sharpening of the traditional legal and ethical dilemmas, in particular those between the freedom of expression and the necessity of control. Therefore, along with the increasing complexity of social relations, the reliability of the regulations comes from being based on the universal, real and rational foundation of natural law, recognized in the classical philosophical tradition.[16] Therefore, reference to other assumptions – idealistic, subjective and voluntaristic – deepens the chaos and hinders communication. As a result, this will turn against the Internet itself, as it will prevent the expansion of its infrastructure on the global scale and will not allow it to be used for the benefit of all communities.

4. Information revolution in law

From the sociological point of view, Szwed writes that:

> The changes, we are witnessing at present, are associated with the so-called information revolution. While analysing them, we have to see that we are not dealing with the process of evolution, where some stages of development are being substituted by those that follow, but rather with the merging and accumulation of the diverse features of the societies, characteristic for the subsequent stages of their technological development.[17]

[16] One must take into account the following, according to L. Morawski: "The conviction that some manner of conduct is scientific and good, and all the rest is wrong, that methodology can be algorithmed, or at least contained in a common set of rules, has brought more damage than benefits to science. A meaningful example of this is the simply devastating impact of the reconstructionistically oriented methodology with its models, the uncritical belief in the healing power of logic and formalization had on the philosophy of law. And in the end, what is left of them?". In his opinion, methodologists have lost touch with reality because they do not comment upon scientific practice but rather the models of other methodologists. L. Morawski, *Co może dać nauce...* (What can be given to science...), p. 46.

[17] R. Szwed, *Opinia publiczna i pseudoopinie w społeczeństwie zinformatyzowanym* (Public opinion and pseudo-opinions in the informatized society), in: R. Szwed (ed.), *Społeczeństwo wirtualne, społeczeństwo informacyjne* (Virtual society, information society), Lublin 2003, p. 36.

With reference to the Internet, Dobrzeniecki observes that the technical solutions used to build it

> (...) turned out to be factors independent of the political ideologies prevailing in different places on Earth. Their development meant that, on a global scale, the material base formed for some specific values and some special types of social attitudes have become widespread. Along with the increase in new users and the economic importance of the network, the extent of its cultural impact also increased. New types of public discourse have been formed. The Internet had, and indeed has, influence on the development of the tastes and preferences of both the consumers and the voters.[18]

This is why the broad applications of the Internet within law have had an influence on new tasks and the importance of legal data processing. They now refer not only to the local information about law, but also global communication in legal relations.

Dobrzeniecki writes that:

> The information revolution is one of the contemporary phenomena of this type, the complexities of which cannot be managed, save only by applying traditional methods of jurisprudence. Specific properties of information, in combination with the possibilities that are created by the modern information and communication techniques, lead to the formation of phenomena which are extremely difficult to be described by means of the conceptual network of legal positivism. Legal science, in order to respond to this and other challenges of the post-industrial era, must verify some of its assumptions.[19]

Here attention is limited to the analyses of the Polish positive-legal order, because of its leading role in the course of the public informatization activities. Today, activities undertaken for electronization of the creation, application and exercising of law are objects of special interest.

That "classical positivism has already exhausted its internal abilities for self-development and today has nothing interesting to say" was already noted by Lech Morawski in 1999.[20] In his opinion, the crisis of contemporary positivism is as a result of the fact that:

- it turned out to be an ineffective instrument in solving the problems of modern societies, which is demonstrated by the deepening legal nature of social relations and the inflation of legal regulations,
- there is a deep contradiction between its authoritative structure, and the fact that it became one of the most powerful instruments in the

[18] K. Dobrzeniecki, *Lex Informatica*..., p. 57–58.

[19] Ibid., p. 181.

[20] L. Morawski, *Główne problemy współczesnej filozofii prawa. Prawo w toku przemian* (Main problems of contemporary philosophy of law. Law in the course of transformations), Warszawa 2005, p. 16.

democratization of contemporary societies and liberalization of social relations.

Morawski adds that the crisis of classical legal positivism has triggered two, or rather three, attempts at reform, describing the concept of law as the technique and as a conversation, from the systemic and communicative perspective.[21]

> The concept of law as social technique (technological vision of law) may be recognized as a modernistic rationalization of the positivistic model of law. It was, and still is, subject to evolution from traditional model of behavioural regulation, to the model of regulation through stimuli.[22]

The issue of legal data processing discussed here principally refers to the ethical indications of the natural law and the political demands of legal positivism. However, it requires the consideration of contemporary concepts of law which, although they do not explain what law is, comprehensively introduce its operation in the complication of social relations.

On the other hand, Oleński and Jaworski state that the effect of the development of information technologies lies in the national and super-national institutional intervention in the lives of the individuals and all communities.

> Institutions interfere in all spheres of life, regulate behaviour of individual persons, families, social groups, and organizational entities through the detailed orders and prohibitions. The extent of regulation has the total range and the norms refer to all identifiable precise situations, events and processes.[23]

Deep institutional interventionism is the immediate consequence of the development and popularization of modern information technologies. According to the previously cited authors:

> Modern information technologies have made it possible for political institutions to regulate all spheres of individual and public life. They have also made it possible to control observation of the enacted standards. In the condition of contemporary teleinformatic technologies, the possibilities to control observation of the standards by political institutions are incomparably larger.[24]

---

[21] Ibid., p. 17.

[22] Ibid., p. 42.

[23] J. Oleński, W. Jaworski, *Uwarunkowania patologii informacji i drogi jej zwalczania* (Determinants of the information pathology and ways to counteract them), in: W. Góralczyk (ed.), *Prawo informacji: prawo do informacji* (Law of information: right to information), Warszawa 2006, p. 279.

[24] Ibid., p. 280. On the impact of ICT on politics, see: L. Porębski, *Elektroniczne oblicze polityki: demokracja, państwo, instytucje polityczne w okresie rewolucji informacyjnej* (Electronic face of politics: democracy, the state, political institutions in the period of the information revolution), Kraków 2001.

This leads to the construction of technopoly, described by Postman as totalitarian technocracy.[25] It constitutes the realization of the outlook on life giving "priority to scientific thinking, and its technical extension and to the acceptance that technical control over nature and escalation of material prosperity are the principal goals of mankind".[26]

Using McLuhan's observation we can say that technology is a social, psychological and legal continuation of the human body, senses and intelligence. Rothert writes that for McLuhan "the technical environment is not only a passive vessel, but constitutes peculiar and dynamic process to change the thinking and acting of an individual".[27] Technopoly therefore determines subordination of everything to the control of technology, which serves itself (self-reproduction) and in itself finds the final target (self-fulfilment), eliminating all other outlooks on life: "Technopoly is based on the belief that we realize our abilities in the best possible way when we act as machines, that machines in many respects could replace us perfectly. One of the consequences of this belief is the loss of confidence in human opinions and subjectivity".[28] This results in the exclusion of the essential human ability for the overall examination in all dimensions, rational, moral and emotional, for the confidence in the "power of computations". In this context, the connection of the sociology of law with the sociology of technology occurs, as the law and technology are more and more closely connected with social products.

Law and technology are the culturally conditioned products of social processes.[29] Their result is the new, global and network-related legal culture, called the legal culture of the Internet, or the Internet legal culture. Its features are often mutually conflicting, because of the ambivalent ways and directions of using the network. Libertarian trends for the idealization of the Internet have resulted from the original assumptions accompanying is construction, more or less valid until the middle of the last decade of the 20th century. However, a realistic evaluation of the Internet today requires the uniform distribution of stresses on the benefits and hazards which result from its popularization. The Internet from inside, i.e. from cyberspace and virtual space, constitutes an artificial world of influence, area of life, dimension of relations and model of activeness which is much more voluntary, extensive, unexpected and free,

---

25 Compare N. Postman, *Technopol. Tryumf techniki nad kulturą* (Technopoly. The triumph of technique over culture), Warszawa 1995, p. 76.

26 W.J. Bober, *Powinność w świecie cyfrowym...* (Obligation in the digital world...), p. 42. For a more detailed elaboration, see: M. Kaku, *Wizje, czyli Jak nauka zmieni świat w XXI wieku* (Visions, or how science will change the world in the 21st century), transl. by K. Pesz, Warszawa 2000.

27 A. Rothert, *Cybernetyczny porządek polityczny...* (Cybernetic political order...), p. 22.

28 W.J. Bober, *Powinność w świecie cyfrowym...* (Obligation in the digital world...), p. 42.

29 With reference to: M. Castells, *Galaktyka Internetu...* (Galaxy of the Internet...), p. 47.

than that known so far. In this new environment of life, recognition and action, the culture, mores, axiology, ethics and law are being formed from the very beginning.

5. Cybernetic destabilization

The object of the general legal regulation is the isolated complexity of social relations. Today, these relations are coming into existence not only in the physical, but also in virtual reality. Along with the progress of the scientific and technological revolution, more and more often the necessity to change the law appears, caused by the transformation of material reality and the influence of non-material reality.[30] It is already known that the comprehensive and mass application of the information-communicative techniques has led to the irreversible destabilization of the established relations.[31] In this connection, new conflicts and social tensions have emerged. As Dobrzeniecki writes: "Increased demand appears for the prescriptive order, that would ensure greater predictability and definite character of the legal situation of an individual. An essential challenge is to create an institutional environment corresponding to the changes introduced".[32] This task seems to be particularly difficult from the perspective of the migration of human non-material activity from real-space to cyber-space. This means going away from the current real-formal institutionalization and towards virtual and digital institutionalization. Whilst today physical activities are legally important and thus observed and formally documented, after some period of time only the virtually disclosed and digitally documented actions will have such significance. The twilight of the "paper civilization" is now being widely discussed.

We can observe that most of the concepts of the information society and law in the information society make the assumptions of the technological, economic, biological, materialistic, or information determinism.[33] In their light, a human is enslaved by the external conditions of existence or the ex-

---

[30] On difficulties in this scope, compare, e.g.: S. Kotecka, *Realne problemy z wirtualnym dokumentem* (Real problems with virtual document), in: *Prawo teleinformatyczne 2007* (Teleinformatic law 2007), No. 1, p. 83.

[31] A new area of conflict concerns areas of influence in cyberspace. Compare P. Sienkiewicz, *Kryzysy i konflikty społeczeństwa informacyjnego* (Crisises and conflicts of the information society), in: A. Szewczyk (ed.), *Problemy społeczeństwa informacyjnego...* (Problems of the information society...), p. 124.

[32] K. Dobrzeniecki, *Lex informatica...*, p. 90.

[33] Technology as a driving force is shown by: Alexander Bard, Jan Söderqvist, in: *Netokracja: nowa elita władzy i życie po kapitalizmie* (Netocracy: new elite of power and life after capitalism), transl. by P. Cypriański, introduction E. Bendyk, Warszawa 2006, see chapter I.

ternal factors co-forming him. But, the mechanism of specifically human activity consists in self-determination, and failing to perceive it undermines the existence of ethics and the sense of the binding nature of law. The *a priori* assumption that good lies in technical progress itself leads to the primacy of the computer over its user and the computer network over the society.

With the lack of a realistic and integral vision of an individual as the creator, possessor and beneficiary of the technology, the words of Ellul have come true and, according to him, this can only be totalitarian.[34] The balance between individualism and totalitarianism is assured by personalism.[35] A personalistic vision of a human, society, politics and law overcomes the dilemmas of determinism and indeterminism resulting from a fascination with technical progress.[36] In light of this, the personal dignity and natural structure of a human is the criterion of comprehension, evaluation and regulation of all activeness. Therefore, at the root of each concept of law, lies an intentionally or unintentionally accepted basic assumption concerning reality. To reduce it at the starting point to one of many dimensions leads to unrealistic constructions, which always explain something do not principally conform with experience and common sense evaluation. As such, they stop describing and explaining the world, which is the purpose of science, but constitute its projection and manipulation, which is the essence of ideology.

The resignation of philosophy and theory of law from the truthfulness of cognition (metaphysics), for consistent thinking (ontology), makes communication and cooperation impossible. The line of principal division runs through the outlook of life, open and directed towards transcendence, or closed and confined in immanence. Human existence is at the same time material and spiritual since humans are immersed in the world of objects and symbols, transcendence and immanence, culture and nature. But the forming legal culture is the culture of global computer networks, the exchange

---

[34] J. Ellul, *Technika – umiejscowienie zjawiska* (Technique – location of a phenomenon), in: A. Siciński (ed.), *Technika a społeczeństwo* (Technique and the society), Vol. 1, Warszawa 1974, p. 285.

[35] We can observe that in the law science various directions of social thought are undertaken, i.e., liberalism, theory of systems or communitarizm, while personalism is omitted as not matching the dominating canon.

[36] Determinism, according to K. Popper, is the view that the structure of the world is of such a nature that we can predict any event, if we only have a sufficiently detailed description of the past events and all the laws of nature. Compare *Wszechświat otwarty* (Open universe), op.cit., p. 23, quotation after L. Morawski, *Co może dać nauce...* (What can be given to science...), p. 27. An indeterministic stance is represented by Jean-François Lyotard. Compare *Postmodernizm dla dzieci: korespondencja 1982–1985* (Postmodernism for children, correspondence 1982–1985), transl. by J. Migasiński, Warszawa 1998, p. 7 and the next. If the general dispute between determinism and indeterminism becomes insoluble, what remains is to be guided by effectiveness and suitability of applying these theories in each individual case.

of electronic documents, anonymous interpersonal contacts, intelligent information operations, artificial program agents, determined environments of activeness and mobile legal relations. Castells claims that there is no division between reality and its symbolic representation. According to him, the experienced reality itself is virtual, because it is perceived through symbols, which give it meaning (they allow a person to realize them). This is why he introduces the new term of real virtuality, designating the virtual image systems (artificial world of images), in which material and symbolic human existence are immersed.[37] Therefore, virtual reality is the reality of imagination, which makes the common support for the information and communication processes in all fields.

Cybernetic space as a new environment for processes (activeness) and the virtual form as the new material of objects (things) has created the incomprehensible perspective and scale of changes which we face today. Teleinformatic networks, impacting on the ease, freedom, speed, frequency, quality and comprehensiveness of contacts in turn affects the ease, freedom, speed, frequency, quality and comprehensiveness of traditionally understood legal relations, both in the layer of learning and the expression of will. The methods of shaping the awareness and the degree of respect for freedom differs substantially in both dimensions. At present, here begins the transformation of the established doctrines of civil, criminal, administrative or constitutional law. Referring to Castells, it will have to consist in building bridges between the real world (the space of places) and the virtual (space of transmissions), in order to avoid the chaos of parallel life in two different dimensions.[38] Amongst others, the point is that in both universes the same human laws are valid, the interpretation and execution of which will be considering the otherness of the environments.

Considering the fact that in cyberspace numerous barriers such as space-time, energy-matter, bio-psyche or socio-culture are being wiped-out, there is the need for neutral and general regulations, an increase in the importance of the functional and purpose of interpretation, a diversification of normal assessments and increased measures of carefulness and interpretation of the declarations of will, and knowledge, in the light of justified expectations. This is not only with regards the Internet, but also the entire global information infrastructure and all digital information techniques, which produce numerous antinomies, divergences of opinions and ambiguities of situations. To give an example, information flow itself has a free and controlled, uncontrolled and monitored, anonymous and identifiable, confidential and open, safe and risky nature at the same time. Thus, regulation of phenomena of that

---

[37] Compare M. Castells, *Społeczeństwo sieci...* (Society of the network...), p. 377 ff.

[38] Ibid., p. 428.

type must be diversified and harmoniously consider the similar application of current regulations, the introduction of separate legal regulations, allowing space for self-regulation and controlled infrastructural regulation.

6. Legal data processing

Contemporary concepts of law, in particular Weber's technological law, Teubner's autopoietic law or Habermas's communication law constitute support for the electronic legal transactions. However, they do not explain what in fact the law is. This was much better clarified in the classical theories of natural law and legal positivism. The phenomenon of the technological destabilization of law is the effect of its instrumentalization, operationalization and proceduralization. Currently, there is a need for a balanced interpretation of law, which takes into account both axiological foundations and technical instruments. The legal data processing being produced today already has in its starting point a vast speculative foundation (general-theoretical) and empirical (detailed-practical). On one hand, it adopts the declarations of the philosophy of law with regards its essence, origin and function, and on the other hand, it utilizes the arrangements of the precise legal sciences concerning the methods, forms and areas of the legal acts. An explanation of the existential structure of law is not the same as a description of the legal phenomena. Information technology does not change the origin, nature and the role of law, but radically modifies its form, binding nature and enforcement. In spite of the changes occurring the law, as with humanity, still remains the same, but is not the same as before. The unchanging nature of law is demonstrated by the philosophical anthropology of law, while changing legal phenomena show the great legal cultures. Legal data processing should be placed in the arena of the technical culture of law.

Law, in its deepest sense, does not amount to the technology of control, negotiation procedures and routes of communication but, to a higher and higher degree thanks to legal data processing, is entangled with it. The technological, procedural and communicative entangling of law is the specificity of the phenomena defined as informatization, digitalization, cybernetization, virtualization, telematization and networking. Electronic legal relations are the technologically advanced, procedurally expanded and communication conditioned ways of shaping electronic legal relations and performing of electronic official acts, supplanting the traditional relations and acts.

The irreversible processes shaping the electronic social, political and economic reality are not always accompanied by reflection on the electronic vision of law. Such a role could have been fulfilled by legal data processing, exceeding the legal informatics, principally focused on the practical benefits of law resulting from the informatization. The point is that the information legal order is more democratic and just than the current order. Progress does not consist of the introduction of something new, but something better. There is no use building up the vast teleinformatic infrastructure, with the meticulous electronization of procedures and automation of legal and official acts, if the natural freedom of humans is restricted and the protection of his or her personal dignity is weakened.

The convergence of contemporary legal cultures in cyberspace consists in the shaping of a global model of the information-wise improved activity of law. A manifestation of this are the UNCITRAL (*The United Nations Commission on International Trade Law*) model acts, the intention of which is to unify and validate electronic information in the legal relations.[39] We can observe that: "More and more often technical terminology appears in legal acts and this should be understood and competently combined with the legal terminology".[40] An example is the legal regulation of electronic signatures, which reveals the interpenetration of different legal cultures, in the course of which the American liberal tradition combines with the more restrictive European (Roman-German) tradition. This is already expressed by the notional equipment adopted for the purpose of the regulation of the individual categories of relations and actions. Marucha-Jaworska writes that: "In American acts, definitions are formulated in a more clear, lucid and simple way, which provides the possibility of being comprehended by an average recipient".[41] In her opinion, this is missing in the Polish and European law on electronic signatures, where definitions are written in technical and unintelligible language and the principle of technological neutrality is only apparently realized because standardizations have been subordinated to PKI (*Public Key Infrastructure*). In contrast to the American law, in these acts there is no definition of the electronic data which are contained in the documents, signatures and other information and electronic operations.[42]

---

[39] Compare the UNCITRAL model law of December 16, 1996 (*Model Law on Electronic Commerce*); of July 5, 2001 (*Model Law on Electronic Signatures*); of November 23, 2005 (*Convention on the Use of Electronic Communications in International Contracting*).

[40] M. Marucha-Jaworska, *Wpływ nowych technologii na przepisy prawa polskiego – 13 lat istnienia podpisu elektronicznego – komentarz z odniesieniem do prawa europejskiego i amerykańskiego* (Influence of new technologies on the regulations of Polish law – 13 years of electronic signatures – commentary with references to the European and American law), in: E. Gruza (ed.), *Dokumenty we współczesnym prawie* (Documents in contemporary law), Warszawa 2009, p. 101.

[41] Ibid.

[42] Neutral in terms of the scope of the application of technology and liberal in the formalization of electronic legal relations, the Anglo-Saxon course (deriving from American law) is in favour of not creating the an electronic form of legal actions, but the equivalent form of a normal written form. In Poland it is represented by W. Kocot, F. Wejman and A. Stoś. On the

7. Conclusion

Richard Susskind states that technologies which are destructive to lawyers do not have to be destructive to their clients[43], e.g., due to the costs of services. Destruction refers to the destruction of current forms and formulas for the legal acting and practicing legal professions. Due to other reasons, destructive legal technologies can turn out to be economically or socially salutary, e.g., by extending access to justice, improving of legal relations, legal services becoming cheaper, overcoming formalisms, restricting of the discretion, releasing from casuistry or uncovering abuses.

New technologies, on one hand, contribute to the improvement of processes, saving costs, and to the efficiency of the utilization of resources but, on the other hand, they lead to schematization, automation, packetization and operationalization. In dams of so called commodization, they cause the shifting of law from the public sphere to the private. To an ever greater degree it is the market, not the state, that has an impact on its actions. These are served by the projects of restructuring, deregulation, liberalization, privatization and commercialization. The potential and position of supranational corporations allows one to formulate a thesis on the privatization of law. This consists in: a) replacing of standards of the generally applicable law with the standards shaped by numerous non-government organizations, b) the disrespect of supranational corporations towards national legislations, c) forcing through global programs to minimize the role of the state, in particular in the economy, d) weakening of state institutions by governments accepting the priority of markets, e) greater innovation of private entities than public ones in the sphere of management and organization.

---

other hand, involved in the application of a single technology (RSA) and restrictive in terms of the scope of the formalization of transactions (PKI) the German-Roman course (deriving from German law) is in favour of establishing a new electronic form of legal acts. In Poland it is represented by Z. Radwański, D. Szostek and M. Jaworska.

[43] R. Susskind, *Koniec świata prawników; Współczesny charakter usług prawniczych* (End of the lawyers world; Contemporary character of legal services), Warszawa 2010, p. 101.

Chapter 2

Problems with the Storing and Presentation of Information

Janusz Opiła and Tomasz Pełech-Pilichowski
AGH University of Science and Technology

1. Introduction

The reality around us is characterized by the importance of information as well as its high value to the public. The information society needs fast and reliable communication. Due to the wide availability of computers, including mobile ones, information and communications technologies are exploited in everyday life (electronic shopping, banking, entertainment, source of knowledge). We are witnessing the digitalization of life.

Regardless of the area of application, the use of computers is based on the processing and storing of data (numbers, digits, characters of different format). Such processing is performed with algorithms and it is based on the transformation of input data into an output one. A data set internally linked may be viewed as information.[1, 2] The information (in fact, information is an indefinable term) is recognized as structured data, the message transmitted, having a simple or aggregated form (note that it is often mistakenly believed that information and data are synonymous).[3, 4, 5] Due to the nature of infor-

[1] PWN Encyklopedia, http://encyklopedia.pwn.pl/ (accessed 27.06.2013).

[2] D.J. Solove, *The Digital Person: Technology And Privacy In The Information Age*, New York and London 2004, p. 1–8.

[3] M. Borda, *Fundamentals in Information Theory and Coding*, Berlin, Heidelberg 2011, p. 53–55.

[4] R. Steven, *Coding and Information Theory* (Graduate Texts in Mathematics), New York 2002, p. 1–3.

[5] J.S. Chitode, *Information Coding Techniques*, Pune 2007, p. 1–8.

mation, the processing of information is based on the processing of information codes and depends on its simple (atomic) or complex (aggregated) form. Such codes, generated with dedicated algorithms, are processed on the lower level as data. The aim is to transform data into information codes and then information into knowledge.

Information processing problems are related to the (1) adequate representation in form of data (information codes; including storing issues) and (2) nontrivial algorithms used to process information (codes) into new information or new way of its information. Such processes depend on the context of information, its complexity, integrity and security. One may say that the specific conditions of information processing are strongly associated with the language, understood not only as an official language but also as a specialized language (business, medical, legal one) for special purposes.[6, 7]

This paper outlines the problems of storing and presenting information in the context of the coding of the meaning of words and signs. Finally, the problems of the permanent preservation of data and information are discussed.

2. Digitalization of meaning

Information is to be understood as *a set of data having some meaning*.[8, 9] A given set of data can have a different meaning to different recipients or even no meaning at all. The light from a lighthouse is crucial for sailors but might just be romantic for tourists on the beach, having no other meaning for them. In this case light/darkness timing, understood as a cyclic time series of light and no-light state periods of time is a form of a (rather complex) *sign*. Thus the same sign (i.e. set of data) can have different meanings to different recipients. In other words, what a given sign designates and what it means depends on the knowledge, expectation and experience of a given recipient.[10] One can say that the sign itself is intrinsically ambiguous (i.e. *underdefined*) and its exact meaning depends on a broadly understood *environment*. The theory of meaning itself and the relation between a sign

[6] W. Cyrul, T. Pełech-Pilichowski, P.T. Potiopa et al., *Problems of automatic processing and analysis of information from Polish legal texts*, in: *Proc. of the FedCSIS*, Wrocław 2012.

[7] Ibid.

[8] J.S. Chitode, *Information Coding Techniques...*, p. 1–8.

[9] D.J. Solove, *The Digital Person...*, p. 1–8.

[10] G. Frege, *On Sense and Reference*, in: *Translations from the Philosophical Writings of Gottlob Frege*, ed. by P. Geach and M. Black, Oxford 1960, p. 56–78, first published in "Zeitscheift für Philosophie and philosophische Kritik", Vol. 100(1892), p. 25–50, http://en.wikisource.org/wiki/On_ Sense_and_Reference (accessed 18.09.2013).

and its meaning introduces an even greater complexity but a full analysis is beyond the scope of this paper.

Nowadays, one may observe a rapidly growing excess of information and this includes legal information. Such an extensive amount of data can be handled only by powerful computers. However, to accomplish this task, prior to processing, information has to be digitalized into sets of relevant data. Digitalization, generally speaking, means the process of evaluating the representation of any physical or mental object as a series of digits. In this form, only data can be handled, for example stored and retrieved and thus *storing of information* involves the *digitalization of information*. As a result, the storing and presentation of information is a problem of the digitalization of meaning.

3. Digitalization

Let us define an **idea** as *everything that one can imagine based on their knowledge and experience*. An arrangement of transferring ideas between two people is multistage. The whole process is roughly depicted in figure 1.

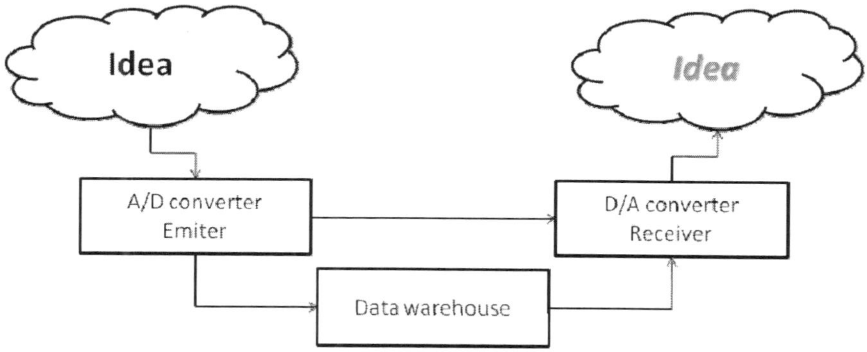

Fig. 1. Simplified communication diagram
Source: own elaboration

Firstly, there is an original idea shown in a "mental cloud" in the upper left corner. Then this idea is converted (A/D converter symbol) from an analogous form into a digitalized form. At the next stage there are two options – data is sent over a communication channel directly to final recipient (upper arrow) or stored in a data warehouse. In both cases the recipient obtains original data which is hopefully unchanged and then converted from the digital back to an analogous form (D/A symbol). Both converters A/D and D/A are usually a unique mixture of apparatus and human skills[11], because an idea prior to A/D conversion has to be expressed in some language and, similarly, post D/A conversion interpreted back from this language. Finally, the original idea is reproduced in the brain of the recipient which is shown as a secondary "mental cloud" in the upper right corner. What is important is that even if data has been transmitted without disturbance through the original communication channel and retrieved, the idea may not match exactly. For example, the word "cookie" may be understood in different ways. First, as a collection of information, usually including a username and the current date and time, stored on the client side by WWW browser, in the form of tiny file in order to retain the information of current browser session state between consecutive visits. Sometimes, malicious websites may try to store illegal and even harmful cookies. The second, the "cookie" is definitely a material object. One can make a photo or even 3D numerical triangular surface mapping to store its digital representation.

So how to efficiently and uniquely digitalize the notion of a cake, store it in a data warehouse and then restore to exactly the same *meaning*? And how to deal with abstract nouns like *love*, *hate*, *crime* or *justice* which do not have a material representation?

The answer seems to be simple – just to name a few of them! Unfortunately, as shown above, during the naming process one assumes that everyone knows and understands the exact meaning of the name given and thus has the knowledge required to restore the original meaning from stored data. This conclusion leads to another: only skilled and trained people can effectively communicate with each other, especially when interactive (face to face or on-line) discourse is impossible, for example on retrieving data from a warehouse or deducing Text of The Law from legal acts. Another point is that storing and recovering meaning to/from a set of data involves a dedicated algorithm. How is such an algorithm related to data?

4. Data + Algorithm = constants

Computers store data in the form of binary numbers. A binary number is a number written in positional notation with a base (or radix) of '2', so using only two digits '0' and '1'. For example number '5' (*five* decimally) in the binary system is written as '00000101' if one assumes a one byte long compu-

---

11 At very least writing/reading skills, pen and paper as the data carrier.

ter word (i.e. eight binary digits). Eight digits can produce only 256 different combinations, denoting only a limited number of values.

If one wants to store, say, the speed of a moving object, she has to split the whole range of possible values into 256 sub ranges (1 km/h or 1 m/s wide), and then restore them just by their unique number. Unfortunately, when digitalized in this manner and subsequently restored, data is granular! This means not only the loss of accuracy, but also suggests a strict connection between the data and the algorithm of its interpretation.

Fig. 2. An example picture as an illustration of balance between complexity of the algorithm and amount of data to store an handle (thoroughly discussed in text)
Source: own elaboration

The image presented in Fig. 2 is a useful example of a general rule that volume of data and algorithm code remains approximately constant, i.e. little data requires sophisticated algorithm to store information code while simple algorithms generate huge data files. In original SVG vector format (complex algorithm but little data) this picture needs 6982 bytes to store.

However in PNG image format (lossless, simple algorithm, raster bitmap format) at 300dpi it needs 518660 bytes (see Fig. 4), and in non-compressed PNM format as many as 18 366 101 bytes (naive algorithm, but a huge pile of data).

Another impressive example is the coding of a paragraph sign. In this case, the proper restoration of the symbol does not guarantee the assumed reception by the reader.

```
<?xml version="1.0" encoding="UTF-8" standalone="no"?>
<!-- Created with Inkscape (http://www.inkscape.org/) -->
<svg
   xmlns:dc="http://purl.org/dc/elements/1.1/"
   xmlns:cc="http://creativecommons.org/ns#"
   xmlns:rdf="http://www.w3.org/1999/02/22-rdf-syntax-ns#"
   xmlns:svg="http://www.w3.org/2000/svg"
   xmlns="http://www.w3.org/2000/svg"
   xmlns:sodipodi="http://sodipodi.sourceforge.net/DTD/sodipodi-
0.dtd"
   xmlns:inkscape="http://www.inkscape.org/namespaces/inkscape"
   width="1052.3622"
   height="744.09448"
   id="svg2"
   version="1.1"
   inkscape:version="0.48.4 r9939"
   sodipodi:docname="Algor.SVG.svg">
  <defs
     id="defs4">
    <mask
       maskUnits="userSpaceOnUse"
       id="mask3779">
      <path
         sodipodi:type="arc"
         style="opacity:0.77205882;color:#000000;fill:#3a3a3a;fill-
opacity:1;fill-rule:nonzero;stroke:#000000;stroke-
width:19.99946022;stroke-linejoin:round;stroke-miterlimit:4;stroke-
opacity:1;stroke-
dasharray:none;marker:none;visibility:visible;display:inline;overflow
:visible;enable-background:accumulate"
         id="path3781"
         sodipodi:cx="242.85715"
         sodipodi:cy="169.80876"
         sodipodi:rx="285.71429"
         sodipodi:ry="277.14285"
         d="m 528.57144,169.80876 a 285.71429,277.14285 0 1 1 -
571.428587,0 285.71429,277.14285 0 1 1 571.428587,0 z"
         transform="translate(38.800001,19.4)" />
    </mask>
    <mask
       maskUnits="userSpaceOnUse"
       id="mask3873">
      <rect
         style="color:#000000;fill:#3a3a3a;fill-opacity:1;fill-
rule:nonzero;stroke:#000000;stroke-width:16.98360252;stroke-
linecap:round;stroke-linejoin:round;stroke-miterlimit:4;stroke-
opacity:1;stroke-dasharray:none;stroke-
dashoffset:0;marker:none;visibility:visible;display:inline;overflow:v
isible;enable-background:accumulate"
         id="rect3875"
         width="473.11465"
         height="533.77032"
         x="161.37151"
         y="93.550262" />
    </mask>.....
```

Fig. 3. Short excerpt from SVG file defining picture from Fig. 2
Source: own elaboration

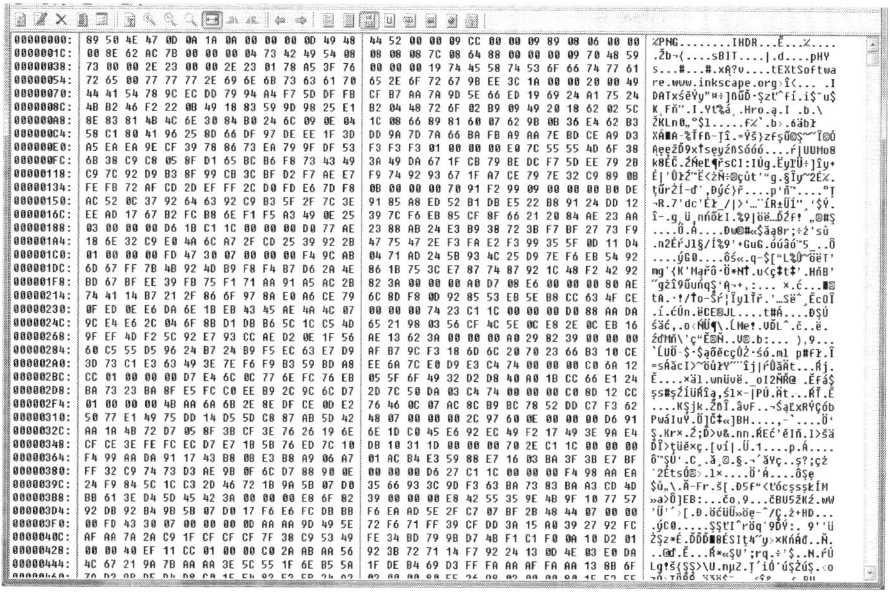

Fig. 4. Binary structure of PNG file.[12] Developed by author
Source: own elaboration

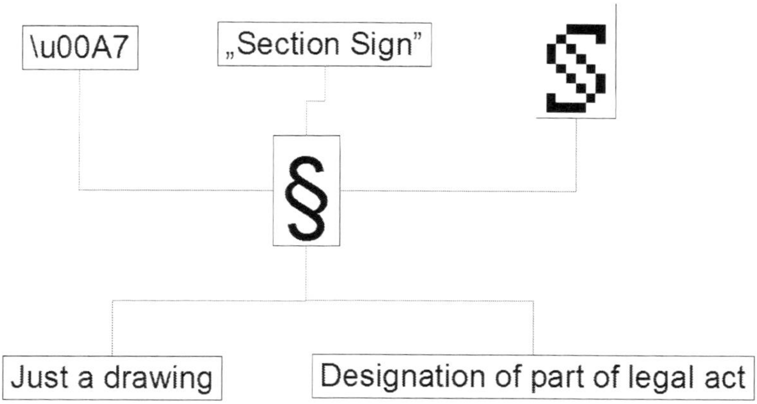

Fig. 5. Variety of representation of the "paragraph sign"[13]
Source: own elaboration

[12] www.FreeCommander.com, freeware (accessed 27.06.2013). Leftmost column numbers of first byte in the row, rightmost column ASCII representation of hexadecimal codes presented in the central panel of the window. FreeCommander viewer screenshot.

[13] In the top row counting from the left representation in: Unicode (method suitable for text processing), then named form (for example met on the Internet in the form of so called *entity*: § or §), mosaic B/W bitmap (fax or dot printer, see Table 1). In the bottom row are the possible meanings for different people.

Table 1. Encoding of paragraph sign as a mosaic of white and black dots. Representation in binary and hexadecimal positional system is given[14]

Row of dots	1	2	3	4	5	6	7	8	Binary notation	Hexsadecimal notation
1	□	□	□	□	□	□	□	□	1111 1111	FF
2	□	□	□	□	□	□	□	□	1111 1111	FF
3	□	□	□	□	□	□	□	□	1111 1111	FF
4	□	□	□	■	■	■	■	□	1110 0001	E1
5	□	□	■	□	□	□	■	□	1101 1101	DD
6	□	■	□	■	□	□	□	□	1010 1111	AF
7	□	■	□	□	■	□	□	□	1011 0111	B7
8	□	□	■	□	□	■	□	□	1101 1011	DB
9	□	□	□	■	□	□	■	□	1110 1101	ED
10	□	□	□	□	■	□	■	□	1111 0101	F5
11	□	■	■	■	■	□	□	□	1000 0111	87
12	□	□	□	□	□	□	□	□	1111 1111	FF
13	□	□	□	□	□	□	□	□	1111 1111	FF
14	□	□	□	□	□	□	□	□	1111 1111	FF
15	□	□	□	□	□	□	□	□	1111 1111	FF
16	□	□	□	□	□	□	□	□	1111 1111	FF

5. Data storage

As it has been shown above, data is just the carrier of information. Information encoded into data can be stored and retrieved but only as long as the data exists. Usually computers handle data internally in the form of specific voltage levels. Unfortunately, this method requires a steady power supply, because just after cutting the electricity supply off the data may disappear. This is why, from the earliest years of computer technology, engineers have sought for an efficient and durable method of permanent data storage which does not require a power supply. In this context, efficiency means a couple of attributes. It is the time required to create a data record and then the time used to restore that data, the so-called access time. Amongst a variety of other factors, one can also mention energetic efficiency, i.e. energy used to store a unit of data for a period of time, dimension and mass of storage device, storage durability, cost of materials and setup. There are also other coefficients depicting

[14] See: W. Cyrul, J. Duda, J. Opiła, T. Pełech-Pilichowski, *Informatyzacja tekstu prawa. Perspektywy zastosowania języków znacznikowych* (*Information of Legal Text*), to be printed.

the quality of a given method or device, for example one of the most important parameters for the evaluation of hard disk drive durability is MTBF, i.e. mean time between failures. Another is the average sequential or random access time which describes how fast a given disk can deliver the required data. In the next section selected storage technologies and devices will be presented including their advantages and disadvantages.

6. Methods of storing data

Punched ribbon and cards

The main principle of both techniques is the same, the only important difference is the shape of the carrier and user friendliness. A punched ribbon is, just as its name suggests, a ribbon made from a special type of durable opaque paper. Recording data involves perforating specific patterns of rounded holes arranged in rows perpendicular to length of the ribbon.[15, 16] One can do this by using a simple manual puncher or employ a more sophisticated electric device. The data written in such a manner is completely unreadable for humans and even skilled engineers have a lot of difficulty in determining what kind of data has been written down – textual , numerical or program. Another bunch of problems arises when the ribbon for some reason requires renovation, both due to damage or mistakes during the punching process. Usually a whole band of ribbon has to be replaced by a new one. The invention of punched cards was a remarkable step in this regard as correction requires the replacement of only the erroneously punched card or damaged cards. Moreover, along the top side of the card, all of the characters encoded on the card were printed and thus were readable for humans. This meant that a large number of cards could be easily inspected when searching for an error in case it had happened.

Magnetic tapes

The invention of magnetic tape storage systems solved many problems connected with punched ribbons but introduced several new ones. Writing to and reading from magnetic tape is fast, but requires the steady movement of tape beforehand of read/write head – i.e. a sophisticated electromagnet. Although the frequency modulation technique allows for a durable and high

---

[15] IBM, *Supplies Division history*, http://www-03.ibm.com/ibm/history/exhibits/supplies/supplies_history.html (accessed 27.06.2013).

[16] Ch. Bovaird, *Before Computers – The Tab Card Epoch*, Danbury Area Computer Society, http://www.dacs.org/archive/0907/feature4.htm (accessed 27.06.2013).

data density level, data written in this method is even harder to read for humans and it is impossible to write it down manually. At the same time, a magnetic tape which is just a plastic ribbon covered by a magnetic layer, is not durable at extreme temperatures. While punched ribbon can even be ironed without risk of data loss (up to 250–300°C), data stored on a magnetic tape can be destroyed at just below 100°C. As magnetic ribbon is usually very thin, it can be twisted, mangled and even torn during readout. Moreover, one of the most annoying drawbacks remaine – the sequential storage system. To read out a piece of data on the end of tape one had to rewind all its length. The most important flaw of magnetic tape design is its susceptibility to the demagnetization process. Magnetic ribbon is tightly wound on a roll, thus almost every piece of tape but the most external is surrounded by two others which are differently magnetized. This, together with thermal excitations in the magnetized layer, leads to the literal vanishing of data.

HDD

To overcome the limitations of magnetic tapes, another magnetic system was designed. Magnetic tape was replaced by spinning a disc, often called a *plate,* which was covered by a magnetic layer and was enclosed together with an electric motor in a durable and hermetic case filled with a neutral gas. Data was written down along concentric paths called cylinders, using powerful magnetic heads. Sometimes several discs were packed together in a single case to increase the overall capacity of the device.[17] Although the first hard disks were rather large, heavy (the size of a washing machine) and very expensive, nowadays they belong to the most reliable, fast and efficient storage devices. Due to the utilization of the giant magnetoresistive effect (GMR)[18, 19], data density reaches even 1 Tbit/in^2 and thus devices able to store more than 1000 GB of data are common.[20] Moreover, as magnetic domains are magnetically aligned perpendicularly to the plane of the disc, durability of the data is greatly enhanced in comparison to magnetic tapes. Data can also been written and read randomly though in small sequentially ordered chunks called sectors. However, HDD's are still prone to data loss at high temperatures and cannot operate at very low (roughly speaking below –50°C, but it depends on the specific design) temperatures. Built-in algorithms refresh magnetic bits thus preventing data loss.

---

[17] See: http://www.tecks.co.uk/technicians/harddrives/harddrives.html (accessed 15.09. 2013).

[18] See: http://searchstorage.techtarget.com/definition/giant-magnetoresistive-effect (accessed 15.09.2013).

[19] See: http://www.gmrsensors.com/gmr-operation.htm (accesed 15.09.2013).

[20] 1 Terabit equals to 1'000'000'000'000 bits, and can be denoted as 1Tb or 1Tbit, see: http://en.wikipedia.org/wiki/Terabit (accessed 15.09.2013).

Optical and magneto-optical disc

The advent of cheap laser technology allowed for the introduction of so--called optical discs. Firstly, this technology was utilized for the distribution of musical recordings in the well-known form of the CD.[21] Once again, the data is stored as a series of dots but this time either reflecting light emitted by miniature laser LED or not instead of holes allowing light through, as in punched ribbon. Despite a lot of progress, such as the introduction of multi-layer DVD or BluRay technology, maximum data density remains lower than in hard discs as well as efficiency in terms of data transfer. Moreover, while a data carrier in hard discs is based on a durable metal plate, optical discs are usually made from more or less mechanically durable plastic prone to destruction at temperatures higher than 150°C. What is more important, data on regular optical disc are read only – after recording, changes are physically impossible. However, this weakness sometimes turns to be a great advantage as it enhances the credibility of stored data.

The magneto-optical variant of this technology allows for the multiple rewriting of data but it is said that due to the magnetical nature of a single bit data stored in this technology can evaporate after some years, thus replication of the discs is required on a regular basis. As a result, this technology turns out to be less reliable as well as more expensive and problematic than HDD technology.

Holographic storage

This is another technology based on the coherency of laser light. Although implemented commercially, it is very expensive and thus its application is limited.[22]

Flash memory

In fact this is a large array of technologies having in common the ability of controlled quasi permanent change of a semiconductor structure. Usually this means the modification of the electrical properties of one of the millions of transistors carved lithographically in a silicon monocrystal.[23] Data can be rewritten multiple times reaching limit of several thousand cycles. One of the greatest advantages of this technology is the durability of the data as bits exist

---

[21] See: E.W. Williams, *The CD-ROM and optical disc recording systems*, Oxford 1994.

[22] R.M. Shelby, *Media Requirements for Digital Holographic Data Storage*, Holographic Data Storage (edt. H.J. Coufal, D. Psaltis, G.T. Sincerbox), Springer Series in Optical Sciences, 2000, Vol. 76, p. 101–111.

[23] See: A. Butterfield, L. Freitas, J. Woodcock, *Mechanising a formal model of flash memory*, Science of Computer Programming, February 1, 2009, Vol. 74, Iss. 4.

as a variant of a physical structure. Its low mass, no more than several grams, makes this kind of mass memory very durable to extreme accelerations allowing it to survive even an airplane crash. Moreover, as it is made from silicon, it is durable at extreme temperatures and data is protected as well thanks to the durability of the case and interface system electronics.

While data density is still lower than HDD's drives and the cost of 1 MB is higher, flash memory has gained a lot of popularity owing to its miniature size, very low power consumption and comparatively high durability.

7. Risks connected with storing of data

Data loss problem

Presently, including stone inscriptions, no method of data storage exists which is absolutely safe, permanent and durable, i.e. resistant to bad environmental conditions like high or low temperature, extreme humidity values, both dry or excessive moisture, or even physical damage caused by fire, water, overvoltage[24] or direct force. The only remedy possible is the implementation of data redundancy. This can be achieved by means of mirroring HDD's (this solution is known as RAID technology) and making backups of data on regular basis. Additionally, a storage plant (sometimes called *data bunker*[25]) should be equipped with sophisticated tools such smoke and fire detectors, automatic waterless fire extinguishers, uninterrupted power supplies, and it should be protected by a trustworthy security agency.

Data accessibility problem

Even very well protected and safe data may become useless if they cannot be accessed in time. Legal content in particular should be available all the time. Lawmakers, judges and lawyers all have to know the current state of the Law to be able to complete their professional mission. For this reason, the communication lines used to transfer data back and forth from a legal data warehouse ought to be duplicated and protected both physically (security personnel, tough equipment) and logically (well designed and tested software, protected against network offenders).

---

[24] This may be triggered not only by natural phenomena such as lightning or a magnetic storm caused by CME, but also intentionally by electromagnetic weapons, EMP (for insights into the problem see: http://www.airpower.maxwell.af.mil/airchronicles/cc/apjemp.html (accessed 01.06.2013)).

[25] A commercial example of a data bunker: http://www.thebunker.net/ (accessed 02.06.2013).

One of the most dangerous method of breaking down services delivered by a data center is the so-called DOS (Denial of Service) or DDOS (Distributed Denial of Service) network attack. Both of them usually employ the generation of an excessive amount of queries for irrelevant data from the server. The difference is that DDOS involves use of myriad of computers, usually previously infected with malicious software, without the knowledge or will of their owners. Thus the sources of the attack are multiple and its true origin barely trackable. Amongst the protection methods one can mention are employment of High Availability Clusters (several computers working in parallel on the same task), firewalls and the filtering of network traffic.

Data integrity – accuracy, correctness and validity

Data integrity may be roughly defined as the property of the identity of retrieved data with original data held in the storage or transmission system as well as the methods ensuring it.[26] The implementation of reliable procedures of checking data integrity is crucial for on-line data storage services. Besides, data introduced into processing system has to be checked to see if it conforms to the input pattern expected by processing programs. This property (called *validity*) can be achieved by means of developing not only regular Boolean rules but also semantic rules or fixed schemas optionally based on XSD formalism. The property of accuracy means that the data refers to actual values under consideration (for example, the stock exchange prices), while correctness refers rather to the data set on the level of the document (for example, a bill or business letter). In order to ensure data integrity qualified digital certificate might be employed. On the other hand, the accuracy of data requires the implementation of policies oriented toward a comparison between original and input data, in this case CRC check function or other error detecting code may be used.

8. Conclusions

The numerical processing of texts aimed at information or knowledge transformation requires a coding method dependant on the processing purpose, input data properties and technical capabilities. For each purpose, both the data representation and storing issues, should be investigated, with a proper analysis of the input data (text), to achieve reliable processing results and to

[26] W. Stallings, *Cryptography and Network Security*, Boston 2010, p. 400–432, 317–340, 377–392.

reduce the risks related to the potential loss of data/valuable information or improper perception of information by the end-user.

The incorrect selection of the media, representation of data/information codes, processing standards, security issues, may lead to data processing uncertainty risks and thus the risk of misunderstanding the message, excessive information noise and, finally, the uselessness of information and communication technologies and resulting inability of meaning digitalization.

The conditions mentioned above are relevant to legal text processing, in particular that which is aimed at automated production of information codes which are unified and recognizable by a target user.

Chapter 3

XML Models for Legal Documents: Current Polish Practices and International Standards

Jerzy Duda
AGH University of Science and Technology

1. Introduction

The legislative processes of legal acts and their promulgation have undoubtedly entered a new area, which is based on the electronic form of creation, storage and information sharing. In the European Union member states are obliged to share public information by Directive 2003/98/EC on the re-use of public sector information (with amendments enacted in 2013). Currently, all countries provide access to national law in the form of HTML pages or PDF files, whereas a widely adopted and accepted format for information exchange on the Internet is presently based on the XML language. The main disadvantage of the traditional approach is the lack of semantic information about the real structure of a legal act and its content which makes a more advanced search in legal texts hardly possible, let alone the application of some knowledge engineering tools. Legal documents are stored locally in national databases, recorded in accordance with the individual, national data structure, and this further complicates the reuse of such documents, especially in a multinational environment. The solution to the above problems is the application of XML language in national legislative processes and the development of a common transnational standard describing the structure of XML documents from national legal systems. It is possible, since in many countries including Austria, Denmark, Italy, the Netherlands, Spain and Poland, legal documents are already prepared in XML format, while similarly there exist some transnational XML standards like Metalex or Akoma Ntoso that can be used in order to describe the structure of national legal acts. The goal of the paper is to discuss the problem of the development of a single national XML standard for legal purposes and its compatibility with transnational standards on the basis of current practices in Poland.

In the following sections basic concepts related to the application of XML language in the legal domain are described, then the most noteworthy examples of XML Schemas for national and transnational legal systems are presented and discussed. Finally the development of an XML legal standard in Poland is analyzed, with special respect to the compatibility of the proposed solutions with transnational standards.

2. XML language and related tools

XML language is currently regarded as the most universal language for data description and sharing in an electronic format. Primarily designed mostly for data exchange between different Internet applications,[1] it has also slowly become a common language for writing various types of documents, including documents created in popular office suites (Open Office, MS Office). The widespread acceptance of the XML standard, almost immediately after its release in 1998,[2] contributed to the postulate of its application also for the documents related to public administration. It is worth noting that XML is not an entirely new concept. The first language that allowed the marking up of a document with tags describing its structure (like headers, paragraphs, tables and so on) was the Generalized Markup Language (GML), developed in the 1960s for IBM. Its descendant – Standard Generalized Markup Language (SGML), originally aimed at sharing documents in large governmental, legal and industrial projects in a human readable form,[3] and approved in 1986 as an ISO norm,[4] became the first publicly available and widely used markup computer language. Both HTML and XML standards are in fact the subsets of SGML standard, much more restricted than its predecessor and targeted for a specific application.

[1] R. Jaideep, R. Anupama, *XML: Data's Universal Language*, IT Professional, May–June 2000, Vol. 2, No. 3, p. 32–36.

[2] XML 1.0 Recommendation was issued by World Wide Web Consortium (W3C) in February 1998, however, the Working Draft has been published earlier, in November 1996.

[3] V. Kashyap, Ch. Bussler, M. Moran, *The Semantic Web: Semantics for Data and Services on the Web*, Berlin, Heidelberg 2008, p. 293.

[4] ISO 8879:1986 Information processing – Text and office systems – Standard Generalized Markup Language.

2.1. Comparison between XML and HTML

The fundamental language for information publishing in the Internet network – HTML – was proposed by Berners Lee in 1991 as a part of an Internet-based hypertext system and originally consisted of 18 tags that could be interpreted by a web browser. In HTML (contrary to XML) tags cannot be extended by a user, so the real structure of the documents cannot be described properly. Fig. 1 depicts an excerpt from the HTML document containing the Constitution of the Republic of Poland published on the website of Polish Parliament.

```
<HTML>
 <HEAD>
  <META HTTP-EQUIV="Content-type" CONTENT="text/html; charset=iso-
8859-2">
   <TITLE>The Constitution of the Republic of Poland</TITLE>
   <link href="../../../style1-2.css" REL="stylesheet"
   TYPE="text/css">
 </HEAD>
 <body topmargin="2">
   <br>
     <BLOCKQUOTE>
    <P ALIGN="CENTER"><FONT COLOR=#A00000><B>THE CONSTITUTION OF THE
    REPUBLIC OF POLAND<BR> OF 2nd APRIL, 1997</B></FONT></P>
    <P ALIGN="CENTER"><B>As published in <I>Dziennik Ustaw </I>No. 78,
    item 483</B></P> [...]
    <B><P ALIGN="CENTER">Chapter I<BR>
    <FONT COLOR=#101084>THE REPUBLIC</FONT></P></B>
    <I><B><P ALIGN="CENTER">Article 1</P></B></I>
    <P>The Republic of Poland shall be the common good of all its
    citizens.</P>
    <B><I><P ALIGN="CENTER">Article 2</P></B></I>
    <P>The Republic of Poland shall be a democratic state ruled by law
    and implementing the principles of social justice. </P>
    <B><I><P ALIGN="CENTER">Article 3</P></B></I>
    <P>The Republic of Poland shall be a unitary State.</P> [...]
   </BLOCKQUOTE>
  </BODY>
</HTML>
```

Fig. 1. First three articles of the Constitution of the Republic of Poland written in HTML
Source[5]

The HTML document presented above contains tags describing the basic structure of the document: quotation <BLOCKQUOTE>, paragraph <P>, ordered list <OL>, and list items <LI>, along with the text formatting tags, informing a browser how to display the contents: bold <B>, italic <I> and

[5] http://www.sejm.gov.pl/prawo/konst/angielski/kon1.htm (accessed 14.06.2013).

font with its color attribute <FONT COLOR>. However, neither the original structure of the legal document is preserved, nor the full description of the legal act is provided.

The main advantage of using XML instead of HTML is the possibility of using any set of tags that can have human readable names and precisely describe the original structure of a document. Fig. 2 presents the same fragment of the Constitution of the Republic of Poland as before, but this time written in XML language.

```
<?xml version="1.0" encoding="utf-8"?>
<act>
   <description status="in force" published="Dziennik Ustaw No. 78,
Item
    483" issue-date="1997-04-02" entry-date="1997-10-17">
    <title> The Constitution of the Republic of Poland</title>
   </description>
   <chapter no="I">
    <title>THE REPUBLIC</title>
     <article no="1">
       The Republic of Poland shall be the common good of all its
    citizens.
    </article>
     <article no="2">
       The Republic of Poland shall be a democratic state ruled by law
    and implementing the principles of social justice.
    </article>
     <article no="3">
       The Republic of Poland shall be a unitary State.
    </article>
     [...]
</act>
```

Fig. 2. First three articles of the Constitution of the Republic of Poland written in XML
Source: own elaboration

Storing a document in an XML format has even more advantages. First of all, there are many tools that can be used in order to process its content for the purposes of knowledge extraction or transformation to any other form of presentation required by the final user. Moreover, XML documents are natively ready for internationalization as they use Unicode standard for character encoding.

2.2. Definition of XML document

The structure of an XML document is usually strictly defined. An XML document, that contains a related definition of its structure (usually in a separate file), can be checked for its "validity".[6] This means that all tags and their attributes have been properly used, i.e. names of the tags are correct, they occur in the right order and are properly nested. Tag attributes are also checked for their names and values. Depending on the document definition standard, other restrictions can be applied for both tags and attributes.

Originally, a document type definition (DTD) standard, based on SGML, was widely used in order to define the structure of XML documents. Fig. 3 shows DTD definition for the fragment of the constitution presented in Fig. 2 (more detailed sections of a legal act, such as paragraphs, points, letters, were intentionally omitted).

```
<!ELEMENT act (description, chapter+)>
<!ELEMENT description (title)>
<!ELEMENT title (#PCDATA)>
<!ELEMENT chapter (title, article+)>
<!ELEMENT article (#PCDATA)>
<!ATTLIST description status CDATA #REQUIRED>
<!ATTLIST description published CDATA #REQUIRED>
<!ATTLIST description issue-date CDATA #REQUIRED>
<!ATTLIST description entry-date CDATA #REQUIRED>
<!ATTLIST chapter no CDATA #REQUIRED>
<!ATTLIST article no CDATA #REQUIRED>
```

Fig. 3. Exemplary DTD schema for a legal act
Source: own elaboration

DTD structure, despite the fact that it uses a specific format of tags, can be relatively easily read by humans. For example, from the DTD document presented in Fig. 3, the hierarchy of sections in a legal act can be read: An act has to contain a description and at least one chapter. A chapter must possess a title and at least one article. An article can contain either data or paragraphs, and finally, paragraphs (if present) contain data. All of the following attributes are required: status, date of issue and date of entry into force for the act's description, and the numbers for the act's subsections.

An XML structure definition in DTD is simple but primarily lacks definition of data types (e.g. a date can be written as any combination of alphanu-

[6] XML documents are checked in two phases. First the document is checked to see whether it is well-formed, i.e. if tags are closed, if they are properly nested, and if the document begins with a single root tag. Next, a well-formed document can be further checked as to whether it is valid against a given structure definition.

merical characters that have no sense in terms of description of some point in time), does not allow for namespaces (e.g. an act as a legal document means something different than act as an action – if they exist in a single XML document without namespaces their meaning is ambiguous). The XML Schema (XSD) proposed by W3C in 2001 was meant to be devoid of these shortcomings, and first of all, it was based on XML language. Fig. 4 shows a definition of a legal act in XML Schema, analogous to the DTD, presented in Fig. 3.

```
<?xml version="1.0" encoding="UTF-8"?>
<xs:schema xmlns:xs="http://www.w3.org/2001/XMLSchema">
   <xs:element name="act">
      <xs:complexType>
         <xs:sequence>
            <xs:element ref="description"/>
            <xs:element ref="chapter" maxOccurs="unbounded"/>
         </xs:sequence>
      </xs:complexType>
   </xs:element>
   <xs:element name="description">
      <xs:complexType>
         <xs:sequence>
            <xs:element ref="title"/>
         </xs:sequence>
         <xs:attribute name="status" type="xs:string"
use="required"/>
         <xs:attribute name="published" type="xs:string"
use="required"/>
         <xs:attribute name="issue-date" type="xs:date"
use="required"/>
         <xs:attribute name="entry-date" type="xs:date"
use="required"/>
      </xs:complexType>
   </xs:element>
   <xs:element name="chapter">
      <xs:complexType>
         <xs:sequence>
            <xs:element ref="title"/>
            <xs:element ref="article" maxOccurs="unbounded"/>
         </xs:sequence>
         <xs:attribute name="no" type="xs:string" use="required"/>
      </xs:complexType>
   </xs:element>
   <xs:element name="article">
      <xs:complexType>
         <xs:simpleContent>
            <xs:extension base="xs:string">
               <xs:attribute name="no" type="xs:byte"
use="required"/>
            </xs:extension>
         </xs:simpleContent>
      </xs:complexType>
   </xs:element>
</xs:schema>
```

Fig. 4. Exemplary XML Schema for a legal act
Source: own elaboration

While allowing for a more precise definition of XML document structure, XML Schema is simultaneously much more complex than DTD. This is why DTD is still used in many cases for the purpose of structure definition of XML files, including the definition of legal documents. In the next section, examples of both DTD and XML Schema used for definition of a legal documents structure will be presented.

2.3. Presentation layer for XML documents

Contrary to the HTML document shown in Fig. 1, the constitution written in the XML document, shown in Fig. 2, contains no tags related to the formatting of the document.[7] It means that an XML document should be accompanied by a file that describes how the XML content must be formatted for display on screen or for printing. This is usually done using XSLT (XSL Transformation) language, which belongs to the wider family of XML tools called XSL (Extensible Stylesheet Language). By executing a script written in an XSLT sheet, the XML document can be transformed into another file format, usually HTML, or indirectly, to PDF file. It is worth noting that an XML document may contain a direct reference to the XLST sheet, and a web browser (or other tool) can use it in order to display the content of XML file, instead of simple displaying XML code, which is the default behaviour. Fig. 5 illustrates a simple XSLT script that produces HTML document on the basis of XML file. The individual sections are formatted in a similar way to the HTML document, presented earlier in Fig. 1.

The XSL family also has yet another language for formatting the content of an XML document which is called XSL-FO (XSL – Formatting Objects). Contrary to the XSLT instructions, XSL-FO tags are placed directly into XML document. This is usually done by executing a specially prepared XSLT sheet after which the XML file must be processed by a special processor, e.g. Apache FOP (Formatting Objects Processor). The final output of this process can be a PDF file, MS RTF, MS Word, or another document format. The process of converting an XML document into PDF format is illustrated in Fig. 6.

[7] Actually, an HTML (or XHTML) document prepared according to the current rules of web pages design should also contain no tags related to formatting, as the presentation layer should be moved entirely to the CSS style sheet written in a separate file.

```
<?xml version="1.0" encoding="UTF-8"?>
<xsl:stylesheet xmlns:xsl="http://www.w3.org/1999/XSL/Transform">
   <xsl:template match="act">
      <html>
      <head> <title/> </head>
      <body>
         <p style="text-align:center;font-weight:bold;color:#A00000">
            <xsl:value-of select="upper-
case(description/title)"/></p>
         <p style="text-align:center;font-weight:bold">
            <xsl:text> As published in </xsl:text>
            <xsl:value-of select="description/@published"/></p>
         <xsl:for-each select="chapter">
            <p style="text-align:center;font-weight:bold">
               <xsl:text>Chapter </xsl:text>
               <xsl:value-of select="@no"/><br/>
               <span style="color:#101084">
               <xsl:value-of select="upper-case(title)"/></span></p>
               <xsl:for-each select="article">
                  <p style="text-align:center;font-weight:bold;
                      font-style:italic">
                      <xsl:text>Article </xsl:text>
                      <xsl:value-of select="@no"/></p>
                  <p><xsl:value-of select="."/></p>
               </xsl:for-each>
         </xsl:for-each>
      </body>
      </html>
   </xsl:template>
</xsl:stylesheet>
```

Fig. 5. Exemplary XSLT sheet transforming part of legal act into HTML document
Source: own elaboration

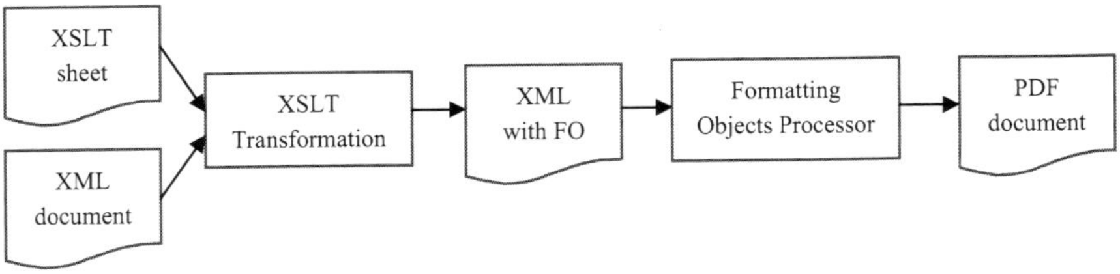

Fig. 6. Conversion process of XML document into PDF file
Source: own elaboration

In a typical scenario, an XML file with embedded formatting objects is intended to be a temporary file, as a result of the transformation of XML document, and this file is usually deleted after the conversion process is finished. The syntax of XML FO vocabulary is complex and this causes XML documents with FO tags to be barely readable by humans. A simple example of such a file that contains the tags responsible for formatting only the page layout and the title section of the legal act is shown in Fig. 7.

```
<?xml version="1.0" encoding="UTF-8"?>
<fo:root xmlns:fo="http://www.w3.org/1999/XSL/Format">
   <fo:layout-master-set>
      <fo:simple-page-master master-name="page" margin-left="2cm"
       margin-right="2cm" page-height="29.70cm" page-width="21cm"
       margin-top="3cm" margin-bottom="3cm">
         <fo:region-body margin-top="1cm" column-count="1"/>
      </fo:simple-page-master>
   </fo:layout-master-set>
   <fo:page-sequence master-reference="page">
      <fo:flow flow-name="xsl-region-body">
         <fo:block font-weight="bold" color="#A00000" text-
         align="center" space-after="5mm">
            THE CONSTITUTION OF THE REPUBLIC OF POLAND
         </fo:block>
         <fo:block font-weight="bold" text-align="center">
            As published in <fo:inline font-style="italic">Dziennik
            Ustaw</fo:inline> No. 78, Item 483
         </fo:block>
      </fo:flow>
   </fo:page-sequence>
</fo:root>
```

Fig. 7. An example of XML file with embedded formatting objects
Source: own elaboration

The main difference between XML and HTML languages is that the former was developed in order to describe its contents while the latter was mainly intended for hyperlinking and presentation. The HTML that is still used in many legal information systems contains no information (at least not in a direct form) related to the structure of the document, or any other additional semantic information (unless it is somehow hidden).[8] An XML document, in turn, usually lacks any information about the presentation layer, thus it should be accompanied with some XSLT file, able to produce the desired output. If the XML documents are intended to be shared among various users (and legal acts definitely are), they should also follow the strict rules of syntax that are defined in DTD or XML Schema file. Otherwise, the original message written by a legislator may be decoded in an incomplete or even wrong way by recipients.

[8] HTML or XHTML file may use class attributes for an indirect structure description. However, class attribute is intended to be used as a selector for CSS, not for semantic purposes.

3. XML language for legal drafting and publishing

Historically, the first legal information systems were created on the basis of popular formats like HTML, RTF, MS Word .doc, ASCII files, and later PDF format, stored directly in a system's database or were generated on the fly from data stored in internal format in such databases (e.g. SQL tables, flat files). For example, in the Legal Information System of the Republic of Austria (RIS[9]) created in 1983, legal acts can be retrieved in HTML, RTF and PDF format. Legal drafts are prepared in MS Word format and stored in a dedicated legislation system called E-Recht. A special plugin for the MS Word editor enables legislators to authenticate to the E-Recht system and to convert Word documents into the XML files that are finally stored in the system. In the future, the XML format will also be used as a retrieval format.[10]

In Europe, the XML standard is currently reported to be used in legal information systems in the Netherlands (SDU BWB), Italy (Norme-In-Rete), Dania (LexDania), Switzerland (CHLexML),[11] and in recent years also in Spain,[12] Estonia, Germany and Ireland.[13] Also European Union Publication Office uses the FORMEX system which, since 2004, has been based on XML language. In the following subsection, the most noteworthy standards will be described.

3.1. National XML standards for legal purposes

The Basiswettenbestand (BWB) legal system contains almost all of the regulations of Dutch law and currently uses the XML format to store legal texts in its database. XML documents must comply with the BWB DTD schema.[14] This schema defines elements able to describe the structure of four main types of

---

[9] Das Rechtsinformationssystem des Bundes.

[10] The e-law project in Austria Electronic support of law-making, Parliamentary Administration Engeljehringer – Schefbeck, Vienna, February 15, 2006, http://www.parlament.gv.at/ZUSD/PDF/2006-04-18_Publikation-Englisch.pdf (accessed 21.06.2013).

[11] An extensive review of XML schemas used in these countries can be found in: C. Lupo et al., *General XML format(s) for legal sources – Estrella European Project IST-2004-027655*. Deliverable 3.1, Faculty of Law, University of Amsterdam, Amsterdam 2007.

[12] D. Blanco, V. Javier, M. González, M. Mercedes, *Spain on Going Legislative XML Projects*, in: C. Biagioli, E. Francesconi, G. Sartor (eds.), *Proceedings of The V Legislative XML Workshop*, European Press Academic Publishing, February 13, 2007, p. 23–38.

[13] LEOS: Legislative Editing Open Software. Final Results, The European Commission ISA, May 2012, https://joinup.ec.europa.eu/sites/default/files/ISA_LEOS_Final_Results_Final_Version.pdf (accessed 21.06.2013).

[14] Current version of the BWB DTD is available at: http://koop.overheid.nl/producten/basis-wetten-bestand/documentatie (accessed 21.06.2013).

Dutch legal documents: law (*wet*) and decision (*besluit*), regulation (*regeling*), circulaire and international agreement (treaty – *verdrag*). The structure of the common element containing either law or decision is shown in Fig. 8.

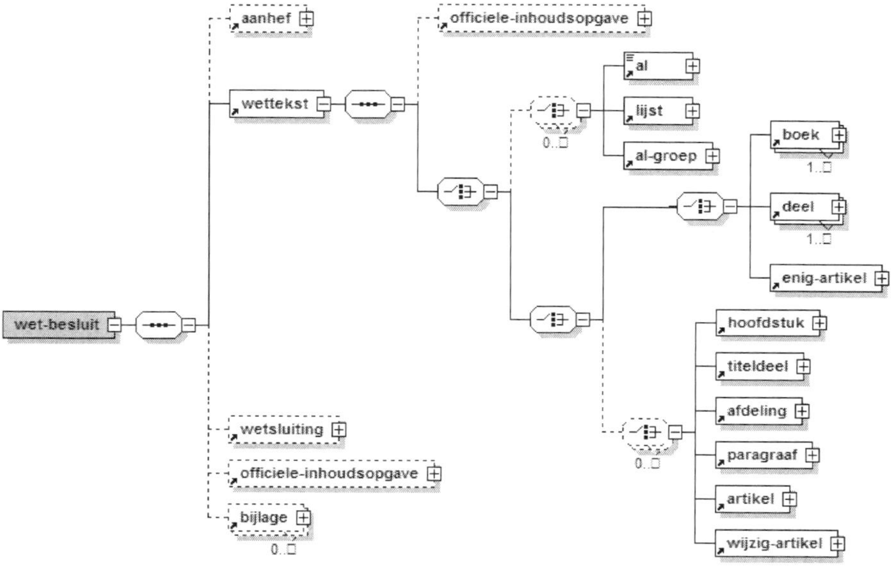

Fig. 8. Schema of *wet-besluit* element from Dutch BWB DTD schema
Source: own elaboration[15]

The main structure of a Dutch legislation document includes: preamble (*aanhef*), the text of law (*wettekst*), closure (*wetsluting*), table of contents (*officiele-inhoudsopgave*) and optional appendices (*bijlage*). The text of law may be organized within books (*boek*), parts (*deel*), chapters (*hoofdstuk*), titles (*titeldeel*), divisions (*afdeling*) and sections (*paragraaf*).[16] Each section may not strictly follow the whole hierarchy and contain articles (*artikel*). Articles can also be written directly without any section. The structure of a simple article in BWB XML consists of paragraphs (alinea – *al*) and lists (*lijst*). The paragraphs next to the text (#PCDATA) may also contain some formatting elements like emphasis (in attributes the exact formatting like bold, italic or caps maybe set), superscript, subscript, underline, and overline.

[15] Visualization prepared in AltovaXML Spy (Home) on the basis of BWB XML DTD schema.

[16] E. de Maat, R. Winkels, T. van Engers, *Making Sense of Legal Texts*, in: *Formal Linguistics and Law 212*, G. Grewendorf, M. Rathert (eds.), Berlin 2009, p. 225–255.

BWB XML also contains tags related to the legislation process and modification of the legal document or its parts. Another group of tags describe the publishing process. In order to manage such a vast number of tags, elements in BWB DTD were grouped into 19 different modules.

A more complex approach to XML schema was applied in the Italian Nome-In-Rete system. The schemas are organized into separate files. There are two DTD schemas used for the definition of a legal document structure – a flexible version (*nirflessibile.dtd*), that is dedicated to the legal acts not following the drafting rules in a circular published on the 20th April 2001,[17] and a strict version (*nircompleto.dtd*), dedicated to a new law. The strict version is more restrictive than the flexible version, but a downward compatible. XML document that is valid according to the flexible DTD schema, is also valid according to the strict DTD schema. Fig. 9 shows the element *NormaNazionale* that describes a national provision in NIR.

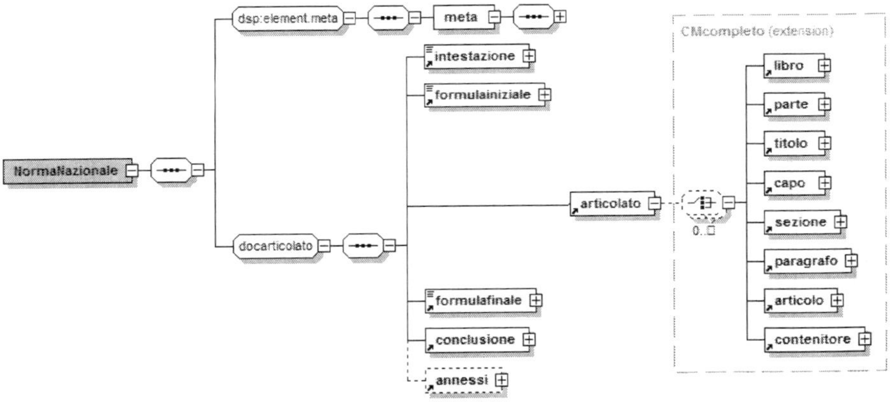

Fig. 9. Schema of *NormaNazionale* element from Italian NIR DTD schema
Source[18]

A national provision (constitution, legislative decree, statutory instrument, regional decree, etc.) is structured with some meta information, introduction (*intestazione*), initial formula (*formulainiziale*), the main articulated content (*articolato*), ending formula (*formulafinale*), conclusion (*conclusione*) and optional appendices (*annessi*). In the strict DTD version, the element *articolato* has to contain sections, that are further organized in a strict hierar-

[17] CIRCOLARE 20 aprile 2001, n. 10888, Regole e raccomandazioni per la formulazione tecnica dei testi legislative (Gazzetta Ufficiale n. 97 del 27.04.2001).

[18] Visualization prepared in AltovaXML Spy (Home) on the basis of CIRCOLARE 20 aprile 2001, n. 10888.

chical order. In the flexible DTD element *articolato* may also be divided into sections, but the strict use of sections (and their order) is not required.

The *nircompleto.dtd* and *nirflessibile.dtd* DTD schemas (in the second version of NIR renamed to *nirstrict.dtd* and *nirfexible.dtd*, respectively) depend on the set of other DTD schemas. All the elements related to the structure of legal act (including *NormaNazionale*) are defined in *norme.dtd*. Among all other DTD schemas, the most important are: *globali.dtd*, that contains the definitions of attributes and elements used throughout other schemas, *testo.dtd*, that contains the formatting elements compatible with HTML, and other tags related to the visualization of a legal document, and finally *meta.dtd*, that contains elements used in the metadata section of the document. Metadata are divided into over thirty groups that include elements related to, for example, the drafting process (*lavoripreparatori*), editorial notes (*redazionale*), publication (*pubblicazione*) and, in NIR2, also related to the life cycle management of the legal document (*ciclodivita*): events (*eventi*) and relations (*relazioni*).[19]

The schemas for Norme-in-Rete are also currently available in the format of XML Schema that are fully compatible with DTD.[20]

3.2. Transnational XML legal standards

In 2000, on the crest of a wave of tremendous interest in the development of the e-economy and creation of standards relating thereto, the OASIS Group, one of the major organizations developing XML standards, established a group responsible for the creation of a common XML standard for various legal purposes called LegalXML. In July 2000 there were over 545 Legal XML members from private companies (50%), government (25%), academic (12,5%), and non-profit organizations (12,5%), coming primarily from the United States.[21] In Europe members were organized within the LEXML initiative, which was established at the legal session of XML Europe conference held in Berlin 2001 (supported mainly by academics from Austria, Germany, Netherlands, Spain, Sweden, and later also Brazil).[22] Many different workgroups[23] were created within OASIS, each responsible for the development

[19] Compare: C. Lupo et al., *General XML format(s) for legal sources...*, p. 22–33.

[20] Linee guida per la marcatura dei documenti normativi secondo gli standard Normeinrete, Agenzia per l'Italia digitale, European Press Academic Publishing, Florence 2012; http://www.digitpa.gov.it/sites/default/files/LineeGuida_marcatura%20documenti%20normativi.pdf (accessed 21.06.2013).

[21] "Todd" V. Winchel, III, *Legal XML and Standards for the Legal Industry*, SMU Law Review, 2000, Vol. 1395, p. 1397–1404.

[22] http://www.juridicum.su.se/lexml/lexml/index.htm (accessed 21.06.2013).

[23] Called formally Technical Committees (TC).

of an XML standard for a different application in the legal domain: Court Filing, eContracts, eNotary, IntJustice (Integrated Justice – for exchanging data in civil and criminal cases), Lawful Intercept, Legislative, ODR (Online Dispute Resolution) and Transcripts.[24] From all of these projects the final XML standards were published only for electronic court filling and electronic contracts. All other projects were postponed.

In 2002 a project called E-POWER was launched, initiated by the Leibniz Center for Law of the University of Amsterdam, in cooperation with Application Engineers and the Dutch Tax and Customs Administration (DTCA), and sponsored by the European Union.[25] One of the outcomes of this project was a MetaLex standard, aimed at being a language and jurisdiction-neutral standard for legislative purposes. The most recent version of Metalex was published in 2010 by the European Committee for Standardization (CEN) as CEN Workshop Agreement no 1571.[26]

The elements of Metalex language are used primarily for the description of a legal documents structure. The current specification of the language includes five types (models) of document content. Text content, similar to HTML, can be written in block elements or inline elements, wherein inline elements can be surrounded by block elements, but not the opposite. Block elements can contain empty elements marking a position in text (*milestone*). Text elements can be grouped into hierarchic container elements (*hcontainer*), that also include a title (*htitle*). The document begins with the root element. The root element and container elements may also act as a container for metadata (*mcontainer*). The structure of the root element in Metalex is shown in Fig. 10.

All elements representing different content type are instances of accompanying abstract elements that can be further extended according to the national legislative system. If the legal act contains, for example, articles in the Metalex language, they can be defined as an instance of a hierarchical container. An example of such a definition that preserves the restrictions defined originally for *hcontainer*, written in XML Schema, is provided in Fig. 11.

As a part of the Estrella project, an XSLT transformation tool for conversion from an Italian NIR DTD to MetaLex was prepared (NIR2Metalex). All 273 NIR elements were converted into Metalex elements, while also metadata were transformed into RDFa attributes. Some special containers, which were specific for NIR, had to be exclusively defined, e.g. general metadata (*gmeta*) for "disposizioni" type of metadata. These metadata can contain text, content elements and other metadata.

---

[24] http://www.legalxml.org/ (accessed 21.06.2013).

[25] http://www.metalex.nl/ (accessed 21.06.2013).

[26] Metalex (Open XML Interchange Format for Legal and Legislative Resources), ftp://ftp.cen.eu/CEN/Sectors/List/ICT/CWAs/CWA15710-2010-Metalex2.pdf (accessed 21.06.2013).

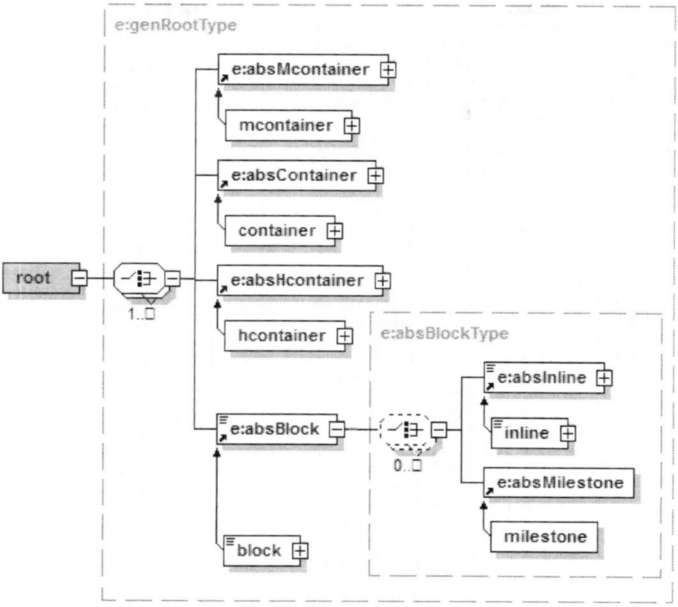

Fig. 10. The structure of root element in Metalex
Source[27]

```
<xsd:complexType name="articleType">
   <xsd:complexContent>
      <xsd:restriction base="e:hcontainerType">
         <xsd:sequence>
            <xsd:element ref="e:absHtitle" maxOccurs="unbounded"/>
            <xsd:choice>
               <xsd:element ref="e:absHcontainer"
maxOccurs="unbounded"/>
               <xsd:element ref="e:absContainer"
maxOccurs="unbounded"/>
            </xsd:choice>
         </xsd:sequence>
         <xsd:attributeGroup ref="e:globnumb"/>
      </xsd:restriction>
   </xsd:complexContent>
</xsd:complexType>
```

Fig. 11. XML Schema fragment defining an article in MetaLex (old version)
Source[28]

[27] Visualization prepared in Altova XML Spy on the basis of Metalex schema available at: http://justinian.leibnizcenter.org/MetaLex/e.xsd (accessed 21.06.2013).

[28] E. de Maat et al., *Translators. (Extended) tools for translating existing other formats into new format*, Estrella European Project IST-2004-027655. Deliverable 3.3, Faculty of Law, University of Amsterdam, Amsterdam 2007, p. 9–10.

For the Dutch law, a system of automatic conversion was developed by Hoekstra.[29] The structure of BWB documents had to be defined using Metalex content type elements, and mapping schema for the elements existing in BWB DTD to the new structure had to be provided. This step was done in a semiautomatic way (some elements in BWB structure had to be defined manually). Finally, the legal documents written in BWB XML could be automatically transformed into the Metalex format, and stored on the server.

In 2004–2005 another transnational legislative language called Akoma Ntoso[30] was developed as a part of the "Strengthening Parliaments' Information Systems in Africa" project, maintained by UN Department for Economics and Social Affairs. Akoma Ntoso was aimed at the development of common standards for parliamentary, legislative and judiciary documents[31] for the Pan-African interoperability of Parliaments. The schema contains one universal root element (*akomaNtoso*), that describes all types of documents: act, bill, judgment, debate, amendment, statement, and other documents and their aggregations or summaries: official gazette, document collection, amendment list, debate report. Some of them (e.g. acts and bills) can have hierarchical structure, some of them (e.g. document, statement) can have an open structure (elements can be included inside other elements in almost any order), while others have the structure related to a particular document type (e.g. amendment or judgment). Fig. 12 shows the structure of act element in Akoma Ntoso, used for legislative purposes. It has a typical, predefined hierarchical structure (similar to the BWB XML or NIR XML structure), that includes: meta, cover page, preface, preamble, the main body of the act, conclusions and attachments.

The body part of the document can use six different patterns for describing its content: *markers* (context-less elements similar to *milestone* in MetaLex), patterns analogous to MetaLex: *inlines* (both semantically relevant inlines and presentation oriented, *blocks* (Akoma Ntoso blocks are based mainly on HTML tags), *containers* (organizing blocks and other containers), and finally *popups* (elements that are out of current hierarchical context, used in mixed model), and *hierarchy* (only one hierarchy with 21 predefined hierarchical elements is used in Akoma Ntoso version 3.0).

---

[29] R. Hoekstra, *The MetaLex Document Server – Legal Documents as Versioned Linked Data*, Proceedings of the 10th International Semantic Web Conference ISWC 2011, Berlin–Heidelberg 2011, p. 128–143.

[30] Akoma Ntoso is an abbreviation for Architecture for Knowledge-Oriented Management of African Normative Texts using Open Standards and Ontologies, in Akan language of West Africa it means "linked hearts".

[31] http://www.akomantoso.org/akoma-ntoso-in-detail/scope (accessed 21.06.2013).

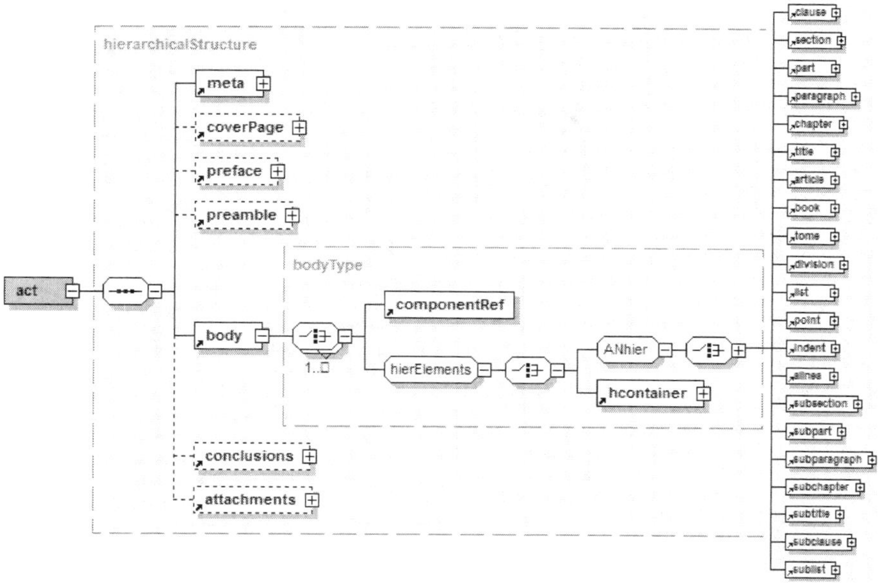

Fig. 12. The structure of act element in Akoma Ntoso
Source[32]

The Akoma Ntoso standard was successfully applied by African Parliaments, but also customized for the legislative purposes of Brazilian Senate (LexML) and European Parliament (XML4EP editor).[33] It also became the basis for OASIS LegalDocML, a new initiative started in 2012, one of whose main goals is "to create a common legal document standard for the interchange of parliamentary, legislative and judicial documents between institutions anywhere in the world".[34]

4. Electronic form of legal acts in Poland

In Poland, the use of ICT in public sector is regulated by the Act of 17 Feb. 2005 on informatization of entities performing public tasks (Dz.U. 2005, no. 64, item 565, as amended). This act adds a new article to the Act of 20 July 2000 on the publication of legislative acts and of certain other acts

[32] Visualization prepared in Altova XML Spy on the basis of Akoma Ntoso scheme available at: http://www.akomantoso.org (accessed 21.06.2013).

[33] M. Palmirani, F. Vitali, *Akoma-Ntoso for Legal Documents, Legislative XML for the Semantic Web Law*, Governance and Technology Series, 2011, Vol. 4, p. 75–100.

[34] A new standard should also be compatible with CEN/MetaLex, https://www.oasis-open.org/committees/legaldocml/charter.php (accessed 21.06.2013).

(Dz.U. 2000, no. 62, item 718), stating that "official journals, collections of local law [...] and other normative legal acts shall be made available free of charge by means of electronic communication" and that "minister in charge of information technology shall determine, by regulation, the technical requirements to be met by means of electronic communication and data carriers used to provide official journals, collections of local law [...]". The Act of February 17, 2005 also introduces the concept of: 1) the minimum requirements for ICT systems used to perform public tasks, 2) the concept of the minimum requirements for public registers and exchange of information in electronic form, and establishes the rules for determining these requirements. Moreover, the act states that these requirements should ensure the openness of information standards. In Appendix 2 to the subsequent Regulation of The Council of Ministers of October 11, 2005 on the minimum requirements for IT systems (Dz.U. 2005, no. 212, item 1766), covering the data formats to provide access to information resources made available through IT systems used to perform public tasks, the following formats determining the structure of the information in an electronic document are listed: XML, XSD (XML Schema), GML (Geography Markup Language used in GIS), and for the transformation of electronic documents: either XSL or XSLT. The newest regulation[35] additionally allows for RELAX NG standard[36] of XML structure description, but first of all, requires technological neutrality of the solutions.

4.1. XML legal standardization in Poland

The Regulation on the technical requirements of electronic documents containing normative acts and other acts, electronic form of official journals and electronic means of communication and information media was finally issued by the Minister of Internal Affairs and Administration on April 25, 2008 (Dz.U. 2008, no. 75, item 451, as amended). According to this regulation, "Electronic documents containing acts being subject to announcement shall be prepared in XML format [...]" and "Acts being subject to announcement in the official journals, collections of local law constituted by district or the municipality shall be published in XML and PDF formats based on XML document". In Annex 5, the detailed XML Schema was provided.[37] Later this schema was updated in 2009–2010, along with the editor of legal acts in XML (called EDAP), developed at the request of the Ministry of Internal Affairs

[35] Regulation of Council of Ministers of May 16, 2012 on the National Interoperability Framework, the minimum requirements for public registers and exchange of information in electronic form, and the minimum requirements for IT systems (Dz.U. 2012, no. 0, item 526).

[36] REgular LAnguage for XML Next Generation (RELAX NG) – another XML schema definition language crated by the OASIS group.

[37] This schema was first contested, and later repealed.

and Administration. The final version of the schema can be found on-line in the Polish public registry Electronic Platform of Public Administration Services (ePUAP).[38]

The EDAP schema defines elements for 13 types of legal documents, including, for example, act, regulation, resolution, judgment or announcement. Fig. 13 shows the structure of act (*ustawa*) element.

Fig. 13. The structure of act (*ustawa*) element in Polish legal schema.xsd
Source[39]

The act element contains metadata (*metryka*), (optionally) a reference to the judgment of the Constitutional Court (*trybunal*), comment elements (*elem-komentarza*), elements describing sections of the act: preamble (*preambula*), part (*czesc*), book (*ksiega*), title (*tyt*), division (*dzial*), chapter (*rozdzial*), article (*artykul*), signatures (*podpisy*), approval (*zatwierdzil*), appendices (*zalaczniki*), footnote content (*tresc-przypisow*), binary appendix (*zalacznik_ _bin*), and finally XML digital signature (XMLDSig – *ds:Signature*). The EDAP schema is stored in a single file and it also does not rely on any other

[38] http://epuap.gov.pl/wps/PA_1_FCHRSKG108KP5023L0FQM82083/produkt_rekomendacji/produkt_rekomendacji_340 (accessed 28.06.2013).

[39] Visualization prepared in Altova XML Spy (Home) on the basis of EDAP schema.

schemas. In this sense it is similar to the BWB DTD schema. However, in contrast to BWB, it forces the sections of the legal acts to be stored in a strict hierarchy, and allows for the better control of types since it is XML Schema.

Along with the EDAP editor ordered by the Ministry, which was developed in platform-independent and open technologies, like Java and Apache Tomcat, commercial editors were prepared by a private company for the MS Windows operating system. These editors use a schema similar to EDAP, however each element has unique identifiers and some of them may have extra attributes (e.g. "repealed" attribute). Fig. 14 contains a fragment of a regulation (*rozporzadzenie*) with *id* attributes for each element, saved in commercial editor.

```
<rozporzadzenie
xmlns="http://www.crd.gov.pl/xml/schematy/edap/2010/01/02"
id="576D21FF-886C-4C9C-BFBC-D171A0F734FD" uchylony="nie"
status="uchwalony" widoczny="tak">
   <!--Legislator 2.1.0.22-->
   <metryka id="DD9848C5-9EDB-4D85-AB98-EC995B4F5AA6" status-
   aktu="uchwalony" nazwa="rozporzadzenie" numer="" opis-
   typu="Rozporządzenie" data="2002-06-20T00:00:00Z" widoczny="tak"
   organ-wydajacy="Prezesa Rady Ministrów" organ-wydajacy-m="Prezes
   Rady Ministrów">
      <organ-wydajacy id="4309074A-8466-44CD-BF7C-A965AA605AFB"
      glowny="tak" w-mianowniku="Prezes Rady Ministrów">Prezesa Rady
      Ministrów</organ-wydajacy>
      <tytul id="25991D03-5B0A-4843-A425-17EAE7420D31">w sprawie
      "Zasad techniki prawodawczej".</tytul>
   </metryka>
   <podstawa-prawna id="F1DB8FC6-6B5C-4EB6-BCA4-F6AD53EC68A5" par="3">
      Na podstawie art. 14 ust. 4 pkt 1 ustawy z dnia 8 sierpnia 1996
      r. o Radzie Ministrów (<link id="AB2C7E1E-CED0-44AF-9663-
      68F484F9648B" typ="hiperlink">Dz. U. z 1999 r. Nr 82, poz.
      929</link>, z<link id="295FA7AD-35DC-4B43-8A8B-9846706A1231"
      typ="hiperlink">2000 r. Nr 120, poz. 1268</link>oraz z<link
      id="74EB4893-34B4-44C1-A86E-63A2DD9E43DA" typ="hiperlink">2001
      r. Nr 102, poz. 1116</link>i Nr<link id="321D17B5-257D-4377-
      A84D-A0E2396B969B" typ="hiperlink">154, poz. 1799</link>i<link
      id="85353E6F-4058-4FD1-A635-71A4BD1CE577"
      typ="hiperlink">1800</link>) zarządza się, co następuje:
   </podstawa-prawna>
   <paragraf id="192E877E-CC68-4457-8F56-C76C626C03C9" nr="1" par="4">
      Ustala się "Zasady techniki prawodawczej", stanowiące załącznik
      do rozporządzenia.</paragraf>
   <paragraf id="80BF31A9-2342-4B59-AF2F-EC285EAD86C2" nr="2" par="5">
      Rozporządzenie wchodzi w życie z dniem 1 sierpnia 2002 r.
   </paragraf>[...]
```

Fig. 14. Internal XML format of legal act in Legislator editor[40]
Source: own elaboration

[40] An extract from documentation and related files for the Legislator editor by ABC PRO.

Although the internal format shown in Fig. 12 can be transformed into the form that does not contain *id* attributes, some attributes like *widoczny* (visible) or *data* (date) in the element *metryka* (acts' metadata) cause that the XML document is still not valid according to the original EDAP schema.

The ambiguities and uncertainties associated with the official EDAP schema meant that this schema was repealed by the Regulation of the President of the Council of Ministers of 27 December 2011 on the technical requirements for electronic documents containing acts and other normative legal acts of the gazettes published in electronic form and electronic means of communication and information media (Dz.U. 2011, no. 289, item 1699). According to this regulation "Electronic documents containing normative acts and other acts being subject to announcement [...] shall be prepared in XML format". This format should be, in turn, consistent with the templates of acts announced in the central repository for electronic document models (part of ePUAP[41] platform). Templates should contain an XSD Schema that is consistent with the structure defined in the Principles of Legislative Technique.[42] Along with the XSD schema, an XSL file determining how to visualize the act should be provided as a part of the template. All the acts being subject to announcement shall be published in PDF format or in XML format, in the way that allows one to visualize its contents in a PDF document.

4.2. XML schema for on-line consultations

Yet another schema was developed within a pilot project dedicated to the on-line consultation system that was fired in 2010 by the Ministry of Economy. The main goal of the project was to increase the transparency of the legislative process, and to involve a wide range of social groups in this process.

The new schema is organized in a similar manner to the NIR XML schema, in which elements were divided into different files, and analogously it has two main versions: *strict*, designed for the preparation of new acts and regulations, and *loose*, that allows the storage of archive legal acts that may not be fully consistent with all the restrictions existing in the strict version. Other types of legal documents, like resolutions and statements, can be structured according to the *base* version of the schema. All these schemas include common elements like text content (*zawartosc tekstowa*), paragraph content (*zawartosc akapitowa*) that are defined in common (*wspolne*) schema. The relations between schemas are depicted in Fig. 15.

---

[41] Electronic Platform of Public Administration Services (ePUAP), http://epuap.gov.pl (accessed 28.06.2013).

[42] Order of the President of the Council of Ministers of 20 June 2002 on The Principles of Legislative Technique (Dz.U. 2002, no. 100, item 908).

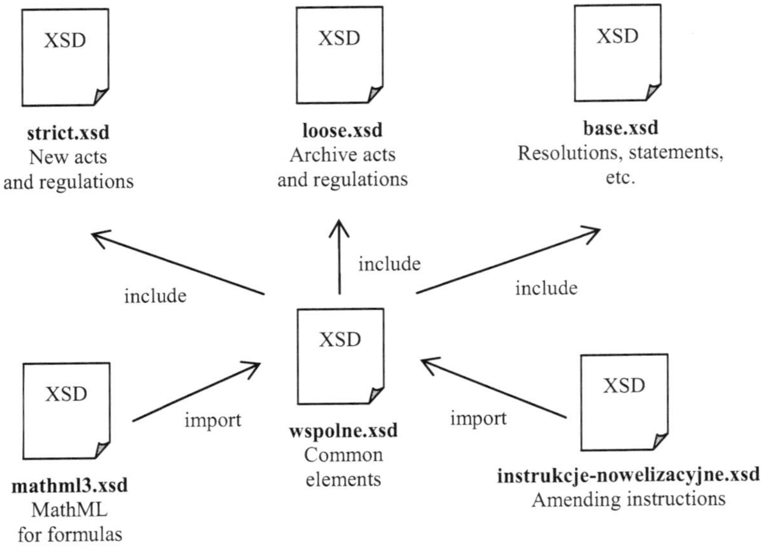

Fig. 15. The organization of schemas in the on-line consultation system
Source[43]

The strict and loose schemas contain 32 elements with two main elements: *ustawa* (act) and *rozporzadzenie* (regulation). Both of these can contain such elements as *data* (date), *tytul* (title), *preambula* (preamble), *zalacznik* (appendix), *artykul* (article – in the case of act), *paragraf* (paragraph – in the case of regulation) and *jednostka-systematyzacyjna* (systemizing, hierarchical unit). As articles or paragraphs are numbered in a continuous way, their content is not placed directly into hierarchical elements (*czesc* – part, *ksiega* – book, *tyt* – title, etc.), but placed on the same level. This is shown in Fig. 16 on the basis of act (*ustawa*) element.

Articles (for acts) and paragraphs (for regulations) can contain enumerations and paragraphs (in editorial sense), that, in turn, can use elements such as text paragraphs (similar to the *p* tag in HTML), tables, raster or vector graphics and equations.

---

[43] *An extract from Dokumentacja techniczna schematów XML Schema opisujących strukturę projektów aktów prawnych w systemie Konsultacje On-line, Warszawa, 20 września 2012 r.* (in Polish), http://www.mg.gov.pl/files/upload/8587/Schemat_XSD_dla%20aktow_prawnych_Konsultacje_On-Line.zip (accessed 28.06.2013).

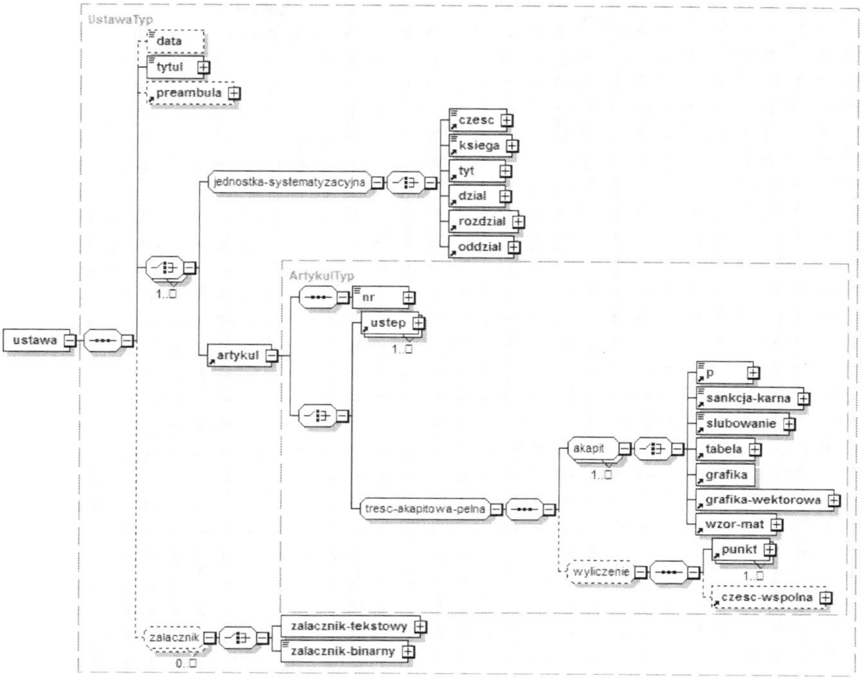

Fig. 16. Act (*ustawa*) element in the schema used in the on-line consultation system
Source[44]

4.3. Polish standards and transnational legal schemas

Further integration within the European Union cannot proceed in isolation from the integration of the legal systems of its Member States. The first step towards such integration should be in the form of a common database of all legal acts that are in force in individual countries. In the majority of these countries, legal acts are currently promulgated in electronic form and, in many cases, electronic documents containing legal acts are treated as authentic and have legal effect (in some countries, including Poland, since January 1st, 2012, they are the only source of new law[45]). Although the European system called N-Lex[46] is able to query national databases according to the

[44] Visualization prepared in Altova XML Spy on the basis of *Dokumentacja techniczna schematów XML Schema...*

[45] As on November 1st, 2011, on-line version of legal gazette are exclusively authentic in: Belgium, Denmark, Spain, Hungary, Netherlands, Austria, Portugal, Slovenia (also in non-EU members: Iceland and Norway), source: Online publication of legal gazettes in Europe (EU/EFTA), http://circa.europa.eu/ (accessed 28.06.2013).

[46] N-Lex was launched on 28 April 2006 and initially covered only 4 countries.

words and value of parameters like the type of act, date of publishing, that are provided by a user, it depends on different API[47] of national legal information systems. As a result, a user cannot always pass all the parameters – e.g. in the Portuguese system, terms to be searched for cannot be inputted, only the number of legal act while for the Czech legal system neither the type of legal act, nor publication date can be provided to the query. Moreover, if the national system does not respond in a given time, the results of the query cannot be displayed. Undoubtedly, a lot more could be achieved if all texts of legal documents could be gathered in one system in the form of XML files that follow a common schema. This would unify and speed up the search process itself, but, first of all, would enable cross searching in legal texts of all EU members, and, in the future, application of different knowledge processing tools which could further facilitate access to legal texts for citizens.

Currently, there is no single standard for legal documents description that is recommended by the European Commission, however, the two standards described in the previous section seem to be the best candidates for such a common European legal standard: Metalex that is currently developed by CEN Committee, and Akoma Ntoso that has been recently adopted for AT4AM editor, used at the European Parliament.[48]

As mentioned before, in the project initiated by Hoekstra[49] on the translation process of Dutch law written in BWB format into Metalex standard, the translation between these two standards in most cases could be done automatically, as all BWB documents follow the same structure. If legal documents do not follow the same schema, the whole process can be much more complex and, as a result, can be affected by many more translation errors.

The document describing the schema developed for the on-line consultation system for the Ministry of Economy[50] contains a short analysis of the conversion capabilities from this schema into Metalex and Akoma Ntoso standards. In the authors' opinion, the most troublesome aspect in the translation process can be vector graphics written in SVG language, equations written in MathML, references for raster graphics and binary appendices saved in external files and, finally, tables (Metalex does not have any dedicated elements for storing tables), and quotations. Similar problems should not affect the conversion into Akoma Ntoso standard.

---

47 Application Programming Interface (API) – the set of rules allowing for interaction with a given system.

48 AT4AM for ALL, the web editor for amending legislation of the European Parliament, is released in Open Source, April 1, 2013, http://www.akomantoso.org/rss-manager/at4am-for-all-the-web-editor-for-amending-legislation-of-the-european-parliament-is-released-in-open-source (accessed 28.06.2013).

49 R. Hoekstra, *The MetaLex Document Server – Legal Documents as Versioned Linked Data...*

50 *Dokumentacja techniczna schematów XML Schema...*

The EDAP schema does not contain elements dedicated for graphics or equations, however, it enables for so-called islands of data, i.e. text fragments that can be placed outside the regular structure of an legal act. This can cause potential problems with translation into Metalex or Akoma Ntoso schema. Other potential problems may result from the definition of events, like the repealing or modification of an act. Both Metalex and Akoma Ntoso allow for the definition of such events in special elements, however, the philosophy behind their construction is different. Fig. 17 indicates, on the basis of preamble element, that only a few elements and attributes can be directly mapped from the EDAP schema to Akoma Ntoso.

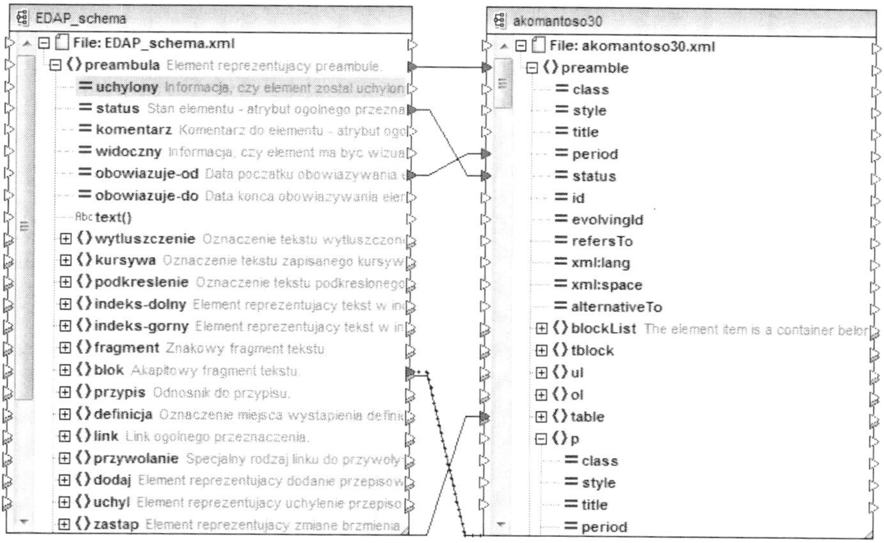

Fig. 17. Preamble element mapped from EDAP schema into Akoma Ntoso schema
Source[51]

Formatting elements that in an EDAP schema can be directly placed under a root element like bold (*wytluszczenie*), italic (*kursywa*), and so on, have to be put in some HTML block element in Akoma Ntoso (e.g. paragraph, list item, and so on). Elements like add (*dodaj*), repeal (*uchyl*) or replace (*zastap*) have to be defined in event or textual modification elements. These and similar difficulties, however, cannot be overcome unless all legal documents strictly follow EDAP or another common schema. If legal documents

[51] Visualization prepared in Altova Map Force on the basis of EDAP and Akoma Ntoso 3.0 XML Schemas.

are defined in XML files with different structure, each type will require an individual definition of conversion procedure and this can be very difficult in practice.

5. Conclusions

In recent years, legal acts and other sources of law have undergone a process of rapid transformation from their traditional paper form to that of electronic documents. The rapid increase in the percentage of citizens having access to the Internet has created the need for such initiatives as freedom of information laws (FOI), as reflected by, among others, in the Electronic Freedom of Information Act Amendments in United States (1996), or in the directive on the re-use of public sector information in the European Union (2003). Legal acts written in an electronic form have steadily replaced the traditional printed form, in many countries becoming the only authentic source of law.

On the other hand, the integration process in Europe and globalization of world economy require instant access to not only national legal documents, but frequently multinational sources of law. Whether it is possible depends on a large extent on the form in which legal documents are prepared and published. The XML language is currently the common, universal format for exchanging information over the Internet network, and allows for the semantic description of legal document content. Although many national and transnational XML standards have been created, there is no single, widely acceptable standard that can be used in the whole legislative process, from legal drafting up to promulgation of the approved act. This is true not only for multinational organizations, like the European Union, but also for individual countries, like Poland. The positive examples of common national standards developed in many countries (e.g. Italy, Denmark, the Netherlands, Switzerland, Brazil or New Zealand), and a multinational standard for African parliaments (Akoma Ntoso) leads one to believe that the development (or adoption) of such standards, and their wide acceptance can be achieved in the near future. This will certainly allow for an entirely new quality to emerge in terms of access to legal information by citizens and the automatic processing of such information.

Chapter 4

Similarity Analysis of Polish Legal Documents Using WordNets Semantic Relations

Piotr Potiopa
AGH University of Science and Technology

1. Introduction

The effective and rapid acquisition and assimilation of information from various sources nowadays constitutes the main factor in both personal and business development. Finding a way for the automatic processing, categorizing, recognition and preservation of useful information is often a determinant not only of undertaking success or project, but more often a requirement assigned for the coming generations.

The aim of this work is to show how the use of the semantic analysis of legal texts is able to improve the quality of information provided by lawyers. This is particularly important in the information society in which we live and, as mentioned above, it is vital for the processing of relevant information.

The legal sources of information in the legal domain and in particular the texts of legal documents are sources which have been checked and confirmed and this permits their rapid and more effective processing. The auto-processing of texts in the domain of Polish law constitutes a crucial role in the aspect of digitalization principles and sources of coherent law.[1] The forma-Aization of legal language can constitute here the factor which minimizes the number of errors related to words relations like polysemy or homonymy

[1] W. Cyrul, T. Pełech-Pilichowski, P. Potiopa, *Problems of automatic processing and analysis of information from Polish legal texts*, in: Proc. of the FedCSIS, Wrocław 2012, p. 939–943.

in existing tools for disambiguation process of Polish texts – in general.[2] We can also use these assumptions in the corpora of legal texts and try to categorize desirable information, to choose what we are directly interested in. Mechanisms of this type can also serve to aid legal information retrieval and thus bring measurable advantages to institutions and companies which need quick and relevant information from available law sources.

In this work, a number of existing tools of the syntactic-morphological (tokenization, stemming and lemmatization) analysis were used to separate lexemes from corpora of legal texts, in this case: TAKIPI tagger.[3] Afterwards, the received data (in the form of separated lexemes) was used in the analysis of the similarity of legal texts with standard methods based on the frequency of representations of occurrence words and on weight techniques, like: TF-IDF and additionally LSI (Latent Semantic Indexing) normalization.[4] Next, the extracted lexemes were analyzed at an angle of mutual similarity of documents forming the spring-corps. Subsequently the WordNET base was used to extract the additional lexemes which are in determined semantic relations with the lexemes separated from the corpus of legal texts. This permitted the comparison of the similarity of calculation results of text documents in the legal domain without the use of semantic relations of lexical units in which such techniques were used.

2. Semantic similarity

Recently many methods of semantic similarity text calculation have been proposed. Many of them determine the specific applications of using semantic similarity analysis methods in the area of artificial intelligence research.[5, 6]

---

[2] D. Ceglarek, *Zastosowanie sieci semantycznej do disambiguacji pojęć w języku naturalnym*, in: T. Porębska-Miąc, H. Sroka (eds.), *Systemy wspomagania organizacji SWO 2006*, Katowice 2006, p. 405–416.

[3] M. Piasecki, *Polish Tagger TaKIPI: Rule Based Construction and Optimisation*. Task Quarterly, 2007, No. 11, p. 151–167.

[4] T. Landauer, S. Dumais, *A solution to Plato's problem: The latent semantic analysis theory of acquisition*. Psychological Review, 1997, Vol. 104(2), p. 211–240.

[5] A. Budanitsky, G. Hirst, *Semantic Distance in WordNet: An Experimental, Application-Oriented Evaluation of Five Measures*, Proc. Workshop WordNet and Other Lexical Resources, Second Meeting of the North Am. Chapter of the Assoc. for Computational Linguistics, 2001.

[6] Y.H. Li, Z. Bandar, D. McLean, *An Approach for Measuring Semantic Similarity Using Multiple Information Sources*, IEEE Trans. Knowledge and Data Eng., July/August 2003, Vol. 15, No. 4, p. 871–882.

After analyzing these methods, it transpired the method outlined below is greatly more effective than the human means for similarity evaluation.[7]

Thanks to the development of projects, which contribute to the construction of national lexical systems of the WordNET type[8] (the Polish WordNET is being developed at Wrocław University of Technology), and their general availability, we have the opportunity to examine the semantic similarity of texts on the basis of the hierarchical structure of information they contain. The cohesion and completeness of this information has a special meaning in the processing of legal texts, where reliable results of automatic text processing count for the evaluation of their efficiency and usefulness.

The proposed method of semantic similarity relies on the measurement of semantic distance between determined words in tree structured WordNET lexemes. This network is organized into a series of synonyms (synsets) which, like lexical units, join with themselves in using semantic relations like: synonymy, hyperonymy, meronymy, fuzzynymy etc.[9] (see Fig. 1 for an example portion).

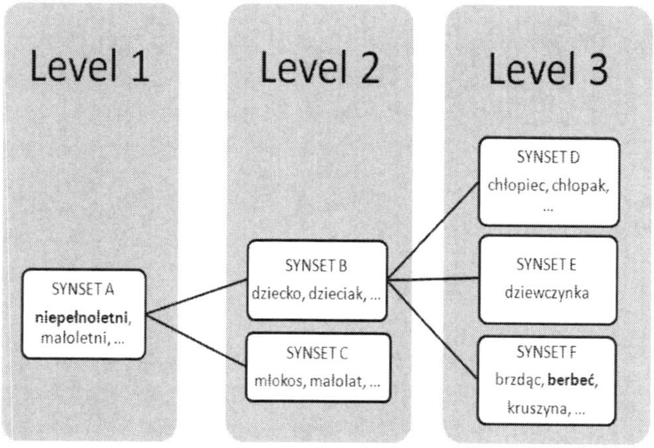

Fig. 1. Example of hierarchical semantic relations based on hyperonymy/hyponymy in WordNET
Source: own elaboration

[7] Y. Li, D. McLean, Z.A. Bandar, J.D. O'Shea, K. Crockett, *Sentence Similarity Based on Semantic Nets and Corpus Statistics*. IEEE Transaction of Knowledge and Data Engineering, August 2006, Vol. 18, No. 8, p. 1138–1150.

[8] M. Maziarz, M. Piasecki, S. Szpakowicz, *Approaching plWordNet 2.0*. Proceedings of the 6th Global Wordnet Conference, Matsue, 9–13th January, 2012, Japan (accepted for publishing); M. Maziarz et al., *Semantic Relations between Verbs in Polish WordNet 2.0*, Cognitive studies, 2011, No. 11, p. 183–200.

[9] M. Piasecki, *Polish Tagger TaKIPI: Rule Based Construction and Optimisation...*, p. 151–167.

As shown above on Fig. 1, the lexeme "berbeć" (*toddler*) is separated from "niepełnoletni" (*minor*) by two semantic relations of hyperonymy (*superiority*). In this way, a semantic distance is defined between the lexemes which are examined.

Having two lexemes w_1 and w_2, semantic similarity ς of w_1 and w_2 is defined as:[10]

$$\varsigma(w_1, w_2) = f(l, h) \tag{1}$$

where l – marks the length of shortest path among lexemes in WordNET network, and h is a depth of the superior lexeme in network of designated for both lexemes: w_1 and w_2. Formula (1) can disintegrate using two functions:

$$\varsigma(w_1, w_2) = f_1(l) * f_2(h) \tag{2}$$

where f_1 and f_2 are appropriately related functions depending on the length of shortest path and the depth of the superior lexeme.

In this work, it has been accepted that the relations generating the semantic similarity of two lexemes in WordNET network will be relations: synonymy, hyponymy, hyperonymy, meronymy, holonymy, and all of the subordinate relations resulting from them. For the construction correctness of the algorithm generating the semantic similarity function, three possible uses were accepted:

1. w_1 and w_2 are found in one synset and are the same parts of the speech;
2. w_1 oraz w_2 are not found in one synset and have common lexemes in their own synsets, and are the same parts of speech;
3. w_1 oraz w_2 are not found in one synset and do not have common lexemes in their own synsets, and are the same parts of speech.

Basing on these foundations, the f_1 function was proposed:

$$f_1(l) = \frac{1}{(1+\alpha l)^{6\alpha}} \tag{3}$$

---

[10] Y. Li, D. McLean, Z.A. Bandar, J.D. O'Shea, K. Crockett, *Sentence Similarity Based on Semantic Nets and Corpus Statistics*. IEEE Transaction of Knowledge and Data Engineering, August 2006, Vol. 18, No. 8, p. 1138–1150.

where α is a smoothing parameter. Function form is that with the increasing length of the shortest path function decreases rapidly. Function f_2 proposed like below:

$$f_2(l) = 1 - \frac{1}{(1+\beta h)^{4\beta}} \tag{4}$$

where β is a smoothing parameter. The function at increasing values h (depths in the structure of the superior lexeme) rapidly grows what we interpret, that more general definitions are higher in the hierarchy of the WordNET network, therefore they are semantically less similar than concepts from the bottom of hierarchy. Considering all of the designated dependencies, the form of the design on the semantic similarity of two lexemes has the form:

$$\varsigma(w_1, w_2) = \frac{1}{(1+\alpha l)^{6\alpha}} \cdot \left(1 - \frac{1}{(1+\beta h)^{4\beta}}\right) \tag{5}$$

Within the calculations framework of the semantic similarity, there was proposed $\alpha = 0.3$ and $\beta = 0.9$ as values best giving "the human" interpretation of the two lexemes similarity. This is achieved by assessing the similarity of the study on a group of several people.

3. Measures and information retrieval model

The vector based information retrieval model (VSM) identifies relevant documents by comparing query terms with terms from a document corpus. The most common corpus weighting scheme is the term frequency (TF) x inverse document frequency (IDF), where TF is the number of times a term appears in a document, and IDF reflects the distribution of terms within the corpus.[11] IDF distribution function is shown below:

$$IDF(w_1) = log2(N) - log2(n_i) + 1 \tag{6}$$

where N is the total number of corpus documents; n_i is the number of documents that contain at least one occurrence of the term w_i ; and w_i is a term, which is typically stemmed.

[11] G. Salton, Ch. Buckley, *Termweighting approaches in automatic text retrieval.* Information Processing & Management, 1988, Vol. 24(5), p. 513–523.

In the described model of the semantic similarity measurement of text documents, a non-standard method of the construction of the terms matrix was applied. The standard method uses the *term-document matrix (TDM)* whilst the proposed method uses: *sentence-document matrix (SDM)* for the purpose of raising the efficiency of the investigation of semantic relations and the best description of dependence between documents. The SDM method is based on counting appearance of terms in documents appearing in particular sentences.

For results comparison the LSI method was also applied to the system. In case of greater data corpora this method examines the matter of dimensionality reduction of the sentence-document matrix.[12] For the sentences/terms, vector similarity measurements were used: Cosine, Jaccard's and Sørensen--Dice measures.

4. Semantic similarity with sentence-frequency

In the proposed calculations, sentences are composed of particular lexemes, separated from the module of the syntactic-morphological processing in processes: tokenization, stemming, lemmatisation, etc. Analysis of the semantic similarity of particular sentences relies on the definition of A-sentence in a document *D-i* about *a* integral lexemes as:

$$S_{Ai} = \{w_1, w_2, \ldots w_a\} \tag{7}$$

Based on this assumption, there is expanded form of sentence S_{Ai} as sentence S'_{Ai}:

$$S'_{Ai} = \{w_1, w_2, \ldots w_a, w'_1, \ldots w'_k\} \tag{8}$$

where $w'_1,\ldots,w'_k$ are new lexemes added to the sentence S_{Ai} on the basis of relations from WordNET database from lexemes of sentence S_{Ai}. Simply, the amount of lexemes in particular document, in which *sentence-by-document* occurrences are calculated, is extended by additional lexemes from WordNET. When counting the occurrences of sentence S_{Ai} the given sentence lexemes are counted in a particular document D-*j* by the methodology:

1. when lexeme *w* originally belongs to the document D-*j*, counter value is 1;

[12] T. Landauer, S. Dumais, *A solution to Plato's problem: The latent semantic analysis theory of acquisition*, Psychological Review, 1997, Vol. 104(2), p. 211–240.

2. when lexeme w originally not belongs to the document $D\text{-}j$, counter appointed by formula (5).

This simplification of the semantic similarity calculation between the sentence and corresponding document has been used to demonstrate the lack of semantic depending on the method of term-frequency. The test results are shown in section 6.

5. Similarity computing architecture

A system architecture, "Fig. 1", was made for the proposed method of counting legal texts similarity which could realize it. In the actual-testing version of system, the basic modules (processing legal text, generating appropriate structures and counting the similarities) were done using Java language and console scripts.

Therefore, on the Fig. 2 diagram, we can distinguish modules:

- XML Preprocessing module – module responsible for processing documents in text form to XML format with determining the division on sentences with terminology ambiguation, resulting from sentences structure and determining of recognized part of speech (for that purpose tagger TAKIPI was used);[13]
- TXT Preprocessing module – the module responsible for the source of documents at an angle of specific for law language structures "(Dz. Urz.WE L 228 z 11.08.1992)", the extraction of acts, preambles and other elements of legal acts according to juridically adopted foundations related with Polish law record standardization;[14]
- Matrix construct & computing – module of the matrix construction *sentence-document* in VSM model and calculating similarity of documents using formulas described in section II and III.

The input of the system is specified as a collection of documents on which the similarity was investigated. The transformation from a collection of documents to a categorized document collection gives us the opportunity to assess which referenced categories are interested in topics that the corpus of collected documents consider.

---

[13] M. Piasecki, *Polish Tagger TaKIPI: Rule Based Construction and Optimisation...*, p. 151–167.

[14] W. Cyrul, T. Pełech-Pilichowski, P. Potiopa, *Problems of automatic processing and analysis of information from Polish legal texts...*, p. 939.

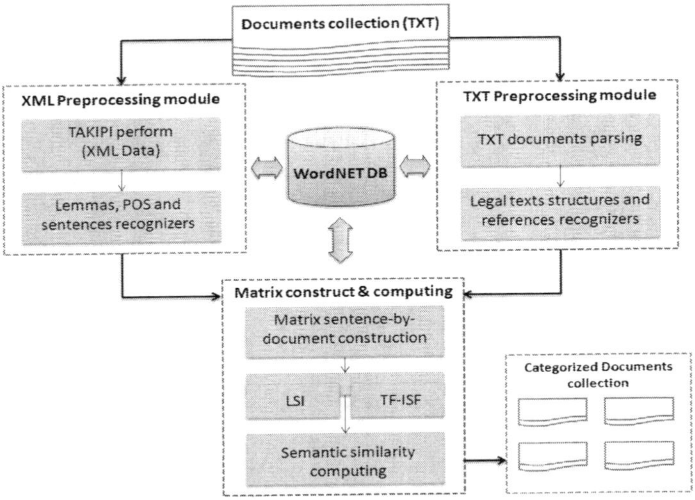

Fig. 2. Schema of architecture system categorizing documents in relation to their semantic similarity
Source: own elaboration

6. Experimental results

The test measures the similarity of testing techniques, mentioned in sections 3 and 4, developed by: standard methods (term frequency) and semantic similarity proposed body of the documents from the legal texts (acts), obtained from the http://isap.sejm.gov.pl website. The legal texts documents was extracted from PDF files officially published on the pages of the Polish government. As a corpus of documents, a set of five Polish legal acts listed below have been chosen: D1: Act on the sale of consumer goods,[15] 14KB (lexemes: 1 559, sentences: 112); D2: Act against unfair market practices[16] (lexemes: 3 439, sentences: 125), 34KB; D3: Act on the protection of consumer rights[17], 27KB (lexemes: 2 725, sentences: 175); D4: An act on the Cinematography Law[18] (lexemes: 4 857, sentences: 327), 48KB; D5: Act on the operations of

[15] Ustawa z dnia 27 lipca 2002 r. o szczególnych warunkach sprzedaży konsumenckiej oraz o zmianie Kodeksu cywilnego (Dz.U. 2002, no. 141, item 1176).

[16] Ustawa z dnia 23 sierpnia 2007 r. o przeciwdziałaniu nieuczciwym praktykom rynkowym (Dz.U. 2007, no. 171, item 1206).

[17] Ustawa z dnia 2 marca 2000 r. o ochronie niektórych praw konsumentów oraz o odpowiedzialności za szkodę wyrządzoną przez produkt niebezpieczny (Dz.U. 2000, no. 22, item 271).

[18] Ustawa z dnia 30 czerwca 2005 r. o kinematografii (Dz.U. 2005, no. 132, item 1111).

cooperative banks[19], 39KB (lexemes: 3 981, sentences: 281). All the collected legal texts have undergone a process of analysis and the extraction of words, which is presented on "Fig. 1".

a. Results for term-frequency based document similarity

Table I. Results obtained with TF/IDF normalization and cosine method

	D1	D2	D3	D4	D5
D1	---	0,0159	0,0382	0,0067	0,0051
D2	0,0159	---	0,0914	0,0109	0,0057
D3	0,0382	0,0914	---	0,0203	0,0273
D4	0,0067	0,0109	0,0203	---	0,0140
D5	0,0051	0,0057	0,0273	0,0140	---
Sum:	0,0658	0,1240	0,1771	0,0519	0,0522

Table II. Results obtained with LSI normalization and cosine method

	D1	D2	D3	D4	D5
D1	---	0,9761	0,8543	0,6696	0,0073
D2	0,9761	---	0,9468	0,8150	0,2244
D3	0,8543	0,9468	---	0,9581	0,5261
D4	0,6696	0,8150	0,9581	---	0,7476
D5	0,0073	0,2244	0,5261	0,7476	---
Sum:	2,5074	2,9624	3,2853	3,1904	1,5055

An application of TD/IDF and LSI normalization with Cosine measure similarity examination method indicates that the document most similar to others is D3 (Table I and Table II), while the most dissimilar to others is D5 (see maximum values of similarity and "summary line"). In the case of mutual similarity of documents from Table I and II, it is shown that D2 and D3 are the most similar to each other, and also show cross-correlations of documents {D2,D3,D4} in the case of the LSI method. That is consistent with "the human" interpretation, because D1, D2 and D3 are documents on consumer rights (Table I and Table II). Slightly strange is the high D4 document similarity to the D3 document in the case of LSI normalization, but we need to confront that with WordNET-relations based similarity measures (as below).

[19] Ustawa z dnia 7 grudnia 2000 r. o funkcjonowaniu banków spółdzielczych, ich zrzeszaniu się i bankach zrzeszających (Dz.U. 2000, no. 119, item 1252).

b. Results for WordNET-relations based documents semantic similarity

Table III. Results obtained with TF/IDF normalization and cosine method

	D1	D2	D3	D4	D5
D1	---	0,7923	0,8804	0,6321	0,5533
D2	0,7923	---	0,8625	0,5782	0,4618
D3	0,8804	0,8625	---	0,6276	0,5587
D4	0,6321	0,5782	0,6276	---	0,5797
D5	0,5533	0,4618	0,5587	0,5797	---
Sum:	2,8580	2,6948	2,9292	2,4176	2,1535

Table IV. Results obtained with LSI normalization and cosine method

	D1	D2	D3	D4	D5
D1	---	0,9635	0,9972	0,8579	0,7013
D2	0,9635	---	0,9805	0,6905	0,4868
D3	0,9972	0,9805	---	0,8175	0,6465
D4	0,8579	0,6905	0,8175	---	0,9678
D5	0,7013	0,4868	0,6465	0,9678	---
Sum:	3,5200	3,1213	3,4417	3,3337	2,8024

After the introduction of the semantic extensions to the SDM matrix (as mentioned in section 4), there are similar results – to the previous term-frequency based similarity computing, but one can see exactly that mutual similarity between documents is focused on D1, D2, D3 documents (Table III and Table IV). This is the expected result because they belong to the same area of Polish law. You can also notice that document D4 is largely similar to other documents used in the analysis, perhaps because it is the largest document in the corpus.

7. Conclusion and future work

According to the documents presented above, the similarity tests results and semantic relations which can be extracted from WordNET systems bring useful information. This information is valuable when testing the similarity of Polish legal texts. Usage of additional calculation models which are more sophisticated than those used in this work may bring better effects. Improvements may be adopted mainly from a range of more precise measurements of the semantic similarity of sentences and testing the semantic sense of lexemes in a sentence. These ideas and proposed techniques may help lawyers and other people to use automatic retrieval and to understand written legal text tools in the Polish legal domain.

Chapter 5

Consolidation of Legal Documents in an Electronic Format

Wojciech Cyrul
Jagiellonian University in Kraków

1. Introduction

Communication shapes legal practices and therefore the implementation into them information and communication technologies (ICT) influences also the way in which law is drafted and promulgated. It leads not only to automation of search and analysis of legal documents, but it opens up as well new ways to manage, visualize and share legal information, and gives new possibilities of work flow control during the legislative process.

Although the implementation of ICT into the legislative process increases its effectiveness, it makes it also dependant on the technological standards used by legislators and their interoperability. Moreover, it entails adjustment of legislative practices to both the requirements and the potential of the new technologies. This is because the informatization of the legislative process involves the development of new tools, which are necessary for making and publishing legal documents in an electronic format, i.e. dedicated editors to tag the texts of legal acts in XML, converters enabling conversion of documents stored in one format to another format, XML Databases to store tagged documents, to manage and verify various versions of legal documents, work flow management platforms for legislative or parliamentary activities and URI/Link resolvers for connection to resources of various lawmaking authorizes.

One of the major changes resulting from the developments and implementation of ICT into legislative processes is the appearance of new ways in which legal documents can be promulgated and consolidated. This is of particular importance in countries like Poland, where legal acts are already promulgated in electronic format, and where in the promulgation of consolidated versions of legal documents one sees a remedy for the information crisis in law.[1]

The consolidation of legal documents is a complex process, usually strictly regulated by law. As a consequence, the way in which legal documents are consolidated can determine the legal status of the consolidated information. For example, while texts consolidated by authorized agents can have official status of the authentic source of law, texts consolidated in a different manner may lack this quality.[2] This situation raises a number of question concerning the status and functions of consolidated legal documents. The fundamental one is, however, whether the more frequent promulgation of authentic consolidated versions of legal texts is able to deal with the reduced clarity of legal texts arising from their numerous and extensive changes and novelizations. Any answer to this question requires one to consider both the nature of regulation concerning legal status of electronic legal documents and the conditions of the informativeness of legal texts. Respectively the following paper discusses selected examples of regulations concerning legal documents in an electronic format and analyses an impact the automatic consolidation of legal documents can have on informativeness of legal texts.

2. Legal status of electronic legal documents. Some European examples

Although the recommendation to use a uniform system to create and make available electronic legal acts was formulated in the Directive 2003/98/EC of the European Parliament and of the Council of 17 November 2003 (Official Journal L 345 of 31 December 2003) on the re-use of public sector information, the development of such systems, however, began in EU countries much earlier. The pioneer of this kind of technology was the Italian Supreme Cassation Court. The system called *Centro di Documentazione Elettronico* – CED, created for this institution, was available for a limited number of courts already at the beginning of the 1970's. Since the early 1980's, more and more documents have been collected in the CED system and the very system became finally available not only for public administration, but also for other

[1] About the information crisis in law see more: F. Studnicki, *Wstęp do informatyki prawniczej (*Introduction to Legal Informatics*)*, Warszawa 1978, p. 16.

[2] The presumption of the authenticity of the legal text, only results in the fact that the legislator shall be liable for the errors contained herein, not the entity that is guided by an erroneous text.

groups of users.[3] Italy is also one of the first European countries which began to make its official journals available on the Internet. These journals have been made available in the official electronic journal GURITEL by Istituto Poligrafico e Zecca dello Stato since 1987, however the documents published on this website did not have the status of an authentic text.[4] In 1999, the Italian Minister of Justice launched a new project for a public legal information system called *Norme in Rete* (norms on the Net), which, among others, led to the development of an outline of the XML document structure of a legal act in the DTD form. This format was published by the governmental agency AIPA (Agenzia per l'Informatica nella pubblica amministrazione) in 2002 and became the standard for recording of legal acts. The guidelines for the outline developed were determined in the Regulation of the President of the Italian Council of Ministers of 20 April 2001 on the principles and recommendations for the technical construction of legal texts *Regole e raccomandazioni formulazione per la tecnica dei testi legislativi*.[5] The standards developed for the *Norme in rete* system made it possible to share the provisions of Italian law on the NORMATTIVA portal, which is the first free Italian public database containing updated, real-time information about applicable law. Still, however, they did not obtain the status of authentic information,[6] which is reserved only for legal texts published both in print and electronic form in *La Gazzetta Ufficiale Italiana*.

Another pioneer in the development of public legal information systems is Austria, which has been developing its own electronic legal information system called *Rechtsinformationssystem des Bundes* (RIS) since 1983. Initially it covered only federal law, then the Supreme Court judicature and now also includes information among others on state (Länder) law, union communities (Gemeiderecht), EU law, court judicature and decrees of federal ministries. It should be underlined, however, that not all of the information available on RIS has the status of authentic information. This status is granted only to the texts of legal acts issued after 2004 in the Federal Law Gazette. In other cases only legal texts available in print in the federal, state or other promulgation journals are regarded as authentic versions. It should also be noted that the project called *E-Recht* was launched by the decision of the Federal Government of Austria already in 2001, and whose goal was to cre-

[3] G. Peruginelli, *Legal Information on the Web: the Case of Italy*, International Journal of Legal Information, 2006, Vol. 34, Iss. 2, Article 11.

[4] A. Andriani, *The Role of the Official Gazette in the Italian experience of collecting and publishing (European, national and local) norms*, European Legal e-Access conference, 2008, http://www.legalaccess.eu/?La-place-du-Journal-officiel-dans&lang=en# (accessed 08.10.2012).

[5] *Regole e raccomandazioni per la formulazione tecnica dei testi legislativi*, Gazette Ufficiale, No. 97, April 27, 2001.

[6] http://www.normattiva.it/static/legal.html (accessed 16.05.2013).

ate a coherent system involving all of the legislative process – from the draft legislation, through its commenting, to its publication in the RIS system. As a result, popular templates for Microsoft Word text editor were created, allowing for the preparation of the contents of legal acts and their further improvement. The texts which were prepared in this way can then be converted to an XML format and electronically signed using a special network module MOA (*Module für Online Applikationen*), and after approval listed in the RIS[7] database. Thanks to this solution, Austria has decided not to issue the printed version of the Federal Official Gazette since the 1st January 2004.

Also the institutions of the European Union relatively quickly began to build a system including a database of legislation of common European law. The staff of the European Commission since 1967 can benefit from the French CELEX system (*Communitatis europeae Lex*), containing treaties, international agreements, secondary legislation, supplementary legislation, documents of the legislative process, the Court of Justice and the Court of First Instance judicature, the national implementation of directives, interpellations and parliamentary questions submitted to the European Parliament, as well as the EFTA documents. This system was made available to the public in 1981 thanks to magnetic tapes, and in 1992 its administration was transferred to the Publications' Office.[8] In 1998, for the publication of the Official Journal of the European Union (until 2003 the Official Journal of the European Communities), an internet system EUR-LEX was launched; the CELEX database was incorporated into it in 2004. Until 2011, however, there was no regulation on the authenticity of the journals published in the EUR-LEX, and the judgment of the Court of Justice of the European Union on the Skoma-Lux company against the Customs Office in Olomouc, confirmed that "such a way to communicate legislation to the public is not tantamount to a valid publication in the Official Journal of the European Union".[9] On 7th March 2013, the Council of the European Union issued a regulation on the electronic publication of the Official Journal of the European Union (Council Regulation (EU) No 216/2013, which entered into force on 1st July 2013). In accordance with article 1, paragraph 2 of this Regulation, official Journal of the European Union published in electronic form is authentic and has legal consequences.

---

[7] B. Barotanyi, *e-Recht – Law Making in a Contemporary Way*, Gazette, 2007, Vol. 1(2), p. 355–360.

[8] *Interinstitutional Style Guide*, http://publications.europa.eu/code/pl/pl-10100.htm (accessed 12.10.2012).

[9] Judgement of 11 December 2007 on the case C-161/06, *Skoma-Lux sro przeciwko Celní ředitelství Olomouc* (Zb.Orz. 2007, p. I-10841), for: Proposal for a Council Regulation on electronic publication of the Official Journal of the European Union 2011/007(APP).

Finally, it is worth mentioning that in many countries today official journals are published only in electronic form via the Internet. This means that legal documents in electronic format have the status of authentic texts. Currently, these countries (apart from Poland) include among others Belgium, Denmark, Spain, the Netherlands, Portugal and Hungary. Most often, however, the status of an authentic text is given both to electronic and printed versions, as is the case for example of Estonia, France, Romania, Great Britain, Italy and Lithuania.[10]

3. Legal status of electronic legal documents in Poland

The main legal act regulating the issues of an electronic version of the legal texts in Poland is the act of February 17, 2005 on the computerization of activity of entities performing public tasks. The act established, among others, the rules for determining the minimum requirements for systems used for the development, exchange and storage of information in electronic form, and created a framework for the development of solutions for the software that allows to connect and exchange information, including sending electronic documents between ITC systems of public entities and systems of entities that are not public entities. The act also determines the principles for the functioning of an electronic platform for public administration services and the central repository of specimen letters in the form of electronic documents.

From the perspective of deliberations on the consolidated text, it is important to note that article 3 of the above act introduces a legal definitions of an electronic document (§2) and a computer data carrier (§3). Accordingly an electronic document constitutes an individual semantic set of data arranged in a specific internal structure and stored on a data carrier understood as a material or a device for recording, storing and reading data in a digital form. Regretfully the abovementioned definition of an electronic document can lead to serious misunderstandings. This is so because, contrary to what is suggested, the data themselves do not mean anything. The data is significant information only through the use of an interpretation algorithm. One can then easily speak of a separate set of data arranged in a certain way, but saying that such a set is a separate semantic entity raises a number of doubts, particularly when one considers texts of legal documents.[11] The issue of the

---

[10] Based on: *Government Legal Services of Liechtenstein*, Online publication of legal journals in Europe (EU/EFTA), http://circa.europa.eu/irc/opoce/ojf/info/data/prod/data/pdf/Authentic_electronic_publication-EU-EFTA-20111101.pdf (accessed 12.10.2012).

[11] See W. Cyrul, *Lawmaking: Between Discourse and Legal Text*, in: *Legislation in Context: Essays in Legisprudence*, L. Wintgens (ed.), Hampshire 2007, p. 43–55.

semantic completeness (autonomy) of the text in general and the legal text or the text of a legal act in particular, goes beyond the scope of this study. Nevertheless, it must be remembered that this problem is much disputed both in the science of text,[12] as well as the theory of law.[13]

From the perspective of the status of consolidation of legal documents in Poland, also article 42 of the aforementioned act is of significant importance, since it changed the act of July 20, 2000 on the publication of normative acts and other legal acts. As a result, first a dual system of the promulgation and storage of legal acts was introduced in Poland, and then (with the force into entry of the act of March 4, 2011 amending again the act on publication of normative acts and other legal acts), it was decided that since January 1, 2012, the legal texts should be published, stored and made available in Poland exclusively in electronic form. In the paper version only certified printouts of the official journals are currently stored. The status of the original text is given however to electronic documents. The force into entry of the act of March 4, 2011 meant that Poland joined the group of member states of the European Union who had resigned from the official paper version of the official journals.[14]

The subject of detailed legal regulations in Poland have also become issues of technical requirements that must be met by the electronic documents containing legal texts. This issue was primarily regulated by the Regulation of the Minister of Internal Affairs and Administration of April 25, 2008 on the technical requirements of electronic documents containing normative acts and other acts, electronic form of official journals and electronic means of communication and information data carriers,[15] and later amended by the regulations of the Minister of Internal Affairs and Administration of June 27, 2008[16] and of December 23, 2008.[17] This issue is currently governed by the Regulation of the Prime Minister of December 27, 2011 on the technical requirements for electronic documents containing legal acts and other normative acts of official journals published in electronic form and electronic means of communication and information data carriers.[18] Under this regulation, legal acts are saved as a structured text in the form of a universal text format

[12] See W. Kalaga, *Mgławice dyskursu* (Nebulae of discourse), Kraków 2001, p. 209.

[13] See W. Cyrul, *Wpływ procesów komunikacyjnych na praktykę tworzenia i stosowania prawa* (Influence of communication processes on the practice of making and applying the law), Warszawa 2012, p. 98 ff.

[14] See *Access to Legislation in Europe, Guide to the legal gazettes and other official information sources in the European Union and the European Free Trade Association*, Publication Office of the European Union, Luxembourg, p. 229.

[15] Dz.U. 2008, no. 75, item 451.

[16] Dz.U. 2008, no. 113, item 722.

[17] Dz.U. 2008, no. 232, item 1568.

[18] Dz.U. 2011, no. 289, item 1699.

to record data in electronic XML form, determined by the W3C standard (World Wide Web Consortium). They are made available in PDF format and electronic documents containing their content are marked with a secure digital signature of the entity authorized to adopt the legal act.

According to the current wording of Annex 3 to the Regulation of December 27, 2011, the content of the structured text of a legal act should include: (1) the structure of the legal act, and thus enable the division into parts, books, titles, chapters, sections, divisions, articles, paragraphs, sections, letters and indents; (2) the text of various parts in the act; (3) the titles of the various parts in the act; (4) footnotes with references; (5) comments on the content placed directly in the text or in the margin; (6) external components included in the content (images, tables, etc. stored in separate documents); (7) annexes to legal acts; (8) references to other legal acts; (9) labels for definitions of dictionary terms. With this in mind, and taking into account the fact that the regulation governs the requirements for data formats and means of electronic communication, an automatic consolidation of legal documents should not pose any technical problems if correct, uniform standards existed and would be properly implemented in the legislative process. Potential difficulties can arise only from the fact that the current regulation does not specify a particular XML schema which would define the structures of XML files containing the texts of legal acts.[19] It only requires that the structures are in accordance with the provisions of the Regulation of the Prime Minister of June 20, 2002 on "The principles of legal drafting".[20] As a result, the definitions of the XML document structure in the form of an XML Schema (XSD), are being developed as part of an electronic platform for public services (ePUAP).[21] Although they do not have legal status the state of their development and technical standards adopted by the legislator enable already today a semi-automatic generation of consolidated versions of legal documents in a way that ensures their integrity and security.

---

[19] Previously, these schemes were contained in Annex 4 of the Regulation of the Minister of Internal Affairs and Administration of 25 April 2008 on the technical requirements for electronic documents containing normative acts and other acts, electronic form of official journals and electronic means of communication and information data carriers (Dz.U. 2008, no. 75, item 451). The annex was, however, repealed by the Decree of the Ministry of Internal Affairs and Administration of 23 December 2008 (Dz.U. 2008, no. 232, item 1568).

[20] Dz.U. 2002, no. 100, item 908.

[21] http://www.epuap.gov.pl (accessed 25.06.2013).

4. Consolidated version of legal documents and text's informativeness

While analyzing the status and function of consolidated legal acts, one should consider how the law is made available, a prerequisite for gaining access to legal information and which determines the degree of informativeness of the legal text from the perspective of the user. Based on the detailed analysis of these issues it will be possible to discuss the legitimateness of inclusion in the corpus of the legal text in electronic format of information allowing not only for presenting the exact meaning of the existing regulations, but also for the reconstruction of the normative level of the text, taking into account the normative status of particular regulation.

One of the main functions of consolidated texts is to reflect the legal status in effect at the time. In other words, the informativeness[22] of the consolidated text depends on its ability to provide the reader with information about what the content of a specific legal act is at the moment. The informativeness of the consolidated text depends not only on the content of regulations included in it and its arrangement, but also on the form of its provision.

While discussing the issue of informativeness and the accessibility of law, it is difficult to ignore the fact that one of the specific characteristics of legal texts is their dynamic nature. This is due to the fact that the legal texts are frequently subject to change resulting from the amendment of the provisions contained therein. As a result, in order to reduce the level of uncertainty associated with the dynamic nature of legal texts, traditionally, from time to time competent authorities publish consolidated texts of legal acts to integrate further revisions and amendments into one coherent document. Unfortunately, technological limitations related to printing had by then meant that the creation of a consolidated text was quite a complicated and costly process and thus consolidated texts were rarely issued. There were however more important side effects of promulgating consolidated versions of legal text in print. The traditional way of publication of consolidated texts meant that people who had no expertise how to read it could easily make a mistake. The existence of a consolidated version of the legal text made many non-lawyer readers to act in the belief that it contains the entire regulation, while consolidated texts show only the state of the regulation as of a particular day. Another problem which may be experienced in practice are situations in which people use the consolidated text, forgetting that it is necessary to familiarize themselves with the content of the announcement, which the unified text is enclosed to and which also contains important information. One should

[22] G. Wierczyński, *Editing and promulgation of normative acts. Commentary*, Warszawa 2010, p. 561.

in particular mention here the information on legal acts, which regulations have in an explicit or formal way introduced amendments to the act which consolidated text is published, information about the verdicts of the Constitutional Tribunal and information on the regulations of the act, which are not included within the consolidated text.

Clearly, the traditional form of the creation and publication of consolidated texts requires particular competence from the reader to use them. Thus it may be argued that the informativeness of a consolidated text determines its intentional effectiveness. As a result, the consolidated text must include not only information which is new to the recipient, but also all of the information which is necessary to ensure that the message can be correctly understood and used. In practice, this means that the amount and type of information which must be included in the consolidated text so that it can meet their basic communication functions as much as possible, depends not only on the legislature, but also on the recipient of text. The presentation of the consolidated text must therefore be adapted to the user's knowledge. A lack or excess of available information may reduce the intentional effectiveness of law. In particular, the lack of specific information may prevent proper understanding and evaluation of the information contained in the text of a consolidated legal act, and the redundancy of the provided information can lead to doubts with regards to its interpretation.

The electronic format allows one to consider the problem of the informativeness of a legal text, in particular the consolidated text, from another perspective. In contrast to the printed text, one in electronic form allows for both the use of tools for the analysis of long texts, taking into account their full complexity,[23] and adjust the amount and type of information displayed on the screen to the user's needs. The electronic format of the text allows for the managing of information in a manner that eliminates information which the user deems irrelevant or the generation and sharing of information of a specific type, for certain classes of users. The electronic form of the text also allows for the use of various search engines or intelligent agents which help users when searching for specific information. As a result of switching to an electronic format, the legislator, to the extent that it does not compromise the integrity of the legal texts, should try to provide information on the law in a way that the recipient can easily find what (s)he is looking for. This in turn is associated with the issues of information management methods, the ergonomics of the interface and the manner of the presentation of information.

The problem of the informativeness of legal texts is of particular importance due to their special status and communication purpose. The informa-

---

[23] M.R. Susskind, *The Future of Law. Facing the Challenges of Information Technology*, Oxford 1996, p. 107 ff.

tiveness of legal texts determines, on one hand, the possibility of enforcement of the basic functions of law, on the other hand, however, is dependent on the degree of saturation of the members of the community with the information about the law as Studnicki[24] has already highlighted. Therefore, discussing the scope of information that should be disclosed in a consolidated text of a legal act one should first distinguish between the informativeness of the law in an absolute sense and in a relative sense. In an absolute sense, the informativeness of the law is associated with the issues of its normative completeness, so the issue of regulation completeness. In other words, the legal text is informative in the absolute sense as long, as there are no gaps. Any factual legal information gap reduces the degree of informativeness of the legal text. However, in a relative sense, the informativeness of the legal text is its ability to provide different recipients with the information they need to perform their roles or to carry out their business. One may easily note that the institution of the consolidated text, just as the internal and external arrangement of information in the texts of normative acts, is associated with informativeness of the law in a relative sense. It should be also noted that in the case of the printed forms of legal texts the improvement in informativeness in an absolute sense does not have to automatically improve the informativeness of a legal text right in a relative sense, and vice versa. The excessive casuistry of regulations can reduce the degree of user's accessibility to information, and in turn any attempts to save and organize legal information, so as to enhance its accessibility can result in redundant information in legal texts or in eligibility and interpretation issues.

Based on the foregoing discussion, it is easy to observe that the concept of the informativeness of a consolidated text cannot be identified with the concept of normative completeness. No text of a legal act beyond the legal system is normatively complete. Therefore, when discussing the scope of the disclosed information in a consolidated text, one should focus on the question of relative informativeness. Undoubtedly, a prerequisite for the implementation of this function is that the content of a consolidated text which is made available to the recipient includes all of the elements constituting its integral part. Further information, which does not constitute the corpus of consolidated legal text, but only affects its meaning, should be displayed/made available only if the recipient of the text desires. Excess information of this type, permanently linked to the consolidated text and always displayed to all users with the same text of the legal act, not only leads to serious doubts as to the type of presented information, but also as to why these and not other information, is presented and reduces the readability of the consolidated text. Given the technological opportunities resulting from electronic data recording

[24] F. Studnicki, *Wstęp do informatyki prawniczej...*, p. 14 ff.

and the sharing of legal texts it seems wiser to allow the user to decide what information (s)he wishes to display at the moment. The legislator should only allow him/her to obtain easy access to the information, tools and technology that will raise the efficiency of the recipient's actions. One such solution might be to share the consolidated legal texts online at any date selected by the recipient with the status of authenticity or the possibility to display the verdicts of the Constitutional Tribunal regarding specific regulations. Moreover, solutions of this type, provide a user with up-to-date information on the law, have been known for a long time. Since the 1990's there have been systems which provide not only consolidated versions of legal acts, but also allow for the management of versions of the texts. One of the first systems of this type are ENACT,[25]AustLII,[26] Lovdata,[27] Legifrance,[28] RIS,[29] EUR-Lex[30] or Polish ISAP.[31] However, automatically or semi-automatically generated consolidated versions of legal act made available by these systems do not have the official status of authentic legal texts.

5. Automatic consolidation of legal documents

From a technological perspective, the problem of uniformity of legal texts is related to the issue of their integrity. After all, the consolidated text of a legal act is not only a legal institution, but also a special form of the presentation of legal information. It is a special form in the sense that it has the status of authenticity, just as the text of the original act. As a result, both in case of the consolidated text and the original text, there is a presumption that the form in which it was announced was shaped by the legislator.[32] So in both cases sharing of these texts in electronic format is related not only to the problem of the authenticity of the shared information, but also in terms of its integrity. The authenticity of the legal text will be preserved if the recipient has access to the

[25] Enact is a legislation system used in Tasmania, which allows for the automatic consolidation of legal acts immediately after its entry into force. The technology is based on the database developed by the Royal Melbourne Institute of Technology *Tera Text Database System*. www.thelaw.tas.gov.au/about/enact.w3p (accessed 25.06.2013).

[26] www.austlii.edu.au (accessed 25.06.2013).

[27] www.lovdata.no/, Norwegian legal information system (accessed 25.06.2013).

[28] www.legifrance.gouv.fr/, French legal government bulletin (accessed 25.06.2013).

[29] *Rechtsinformationssystem*, Austrian legal government bulletin, www.ris.bka.gv.at/defaultEn.aspx (accessed 25.06.2013).

[30] www.eur-lex.europa.eu/pl/index.htm, system of legal acts of the European Union (accessed 25.06.2013).

[31] www.isap.sejm.gov.pl (accessed 25.06.2013).

[32] S. Wronkowska, M. Zieliński, *Commentary on the principles of legal drafting of 20 June 2002*, Warszawa 2012 , p. 206.

content which has actually been prepared and made available by the legislator. The authenticity and integrity of the legal text in the format of an electronic document is ensured and only if it is impossible to introduce modifications to the text by an unauthorized person or in way which would not be in agreement with applicable legal procedures.[33] It is important to note that, in contrast to the original text, the consolidated text of the act is merely declaratory.[34] This means that, unlike in the case of the original legal text, whose main communicative objective is authoritative regulation, the consolidated text is to inform readers about the current state of legal regulation. The difference in the communicative function for both types of legal texts is reflected in the rules for the establishment and functioning of these both forms of presentation of the act. It should be remembered that the original text of the act as a result of the amendments or verdicts of the Constitutional Tribunal is fragmented and dispersed, i.e. formally isolated parts of its structure can be found in the texts of the various legislative or other types of legal acts.[35] The promulgation of the consolidated text is merely a way to counteract the negative effects of this process.

Taking into account the previous deliberations, we can see that the use of electronic forms of legal texts requires the construction of electronic legal information systems capable of the automation process of managing changes in the base of legal information. The quality of action of such systems depends not only on the technology used to allow the system to process different types of information contained in the database with regards to its meaning, but also on the functioning of the system itself. The latter is determined by the ability of the machine to generate valid and reliable results, taking into account both the needs of any user of the system, as well as current and potential events that generate changes in the legal texts. Given the importance of these issues below is a brief description of the basic legislative principles thus determining the efficiency of the automated systems of change management in legal texts.[36]

---

[33] This issue is directly related to the issues of data security which, however, due to the aim of this study is beyond its scope. To obtain more information on this subject please refer to J. Stokłosa, T. Bilski, T. Pankowski, *Security of data in information systems*, Warszawa–Poznań 2001.

[34] Preparation of the consolidated text is a purely editorial procedure. Beyond the scope of this process are issues that require validation or decisions concerning the validity, scope or content of consolidated texts of the existing legal regulations. Compare to M. Błachut, W. Gromski, J. Kaczor, *Legislative technique*, Warszawa 2008, p. 118 ff.

[35] S. Wronkowska and M. Zielinski even speak of a "virtual" nature of these changes. As rightly pointed out, introduction of changes to a legal text does not consist in automatic introduction of changes in the original text, but in the addition to the collection of the texts of new legal texts containing amending them provisions. Cf. S. Wronkowska, M. Zieliński, *Commentary on the principles of legal drafting of 20 June 2002*, p. 206.

[36] Cf. M. Palmirani, *Legislative Change Management with Akoma-Ntoso*, in: G. Sartor, M. Palmirani, E. Francesconi, M.A. Biasiotti (eds.), *Legislative XML for the Semantic Web. Principles, Models, Standards for Document Mangement*, Dordrecht 2011, p. 105 ff.

The construction of a consolidated version of the legal text requires proper consideration of the time sequence system of the introduced changes (*the principle of temporal sequencing*). At the same time in the practice of legislation one has to deal with the retroactive or editorial revisions of the regulations which are already in force. Therefore, the system must also be able to recognize and appropriate consideration of such events, in a way that ensures the continuity of the process of consolidation, in accordance with the chronology of changes (*principle of continuity*).[37]

Bearing in mind the needs of entities making validation decisions in the process of law enforcement, consolidated legal texts automatically generated by the system should provide the user with the information of all modifications that have been included in them in a transparent way (*the principle of transparency and traceability*). What is more, both documents containing consolidated texts, as well as documents containing texts or provisions of the acts that have been repealed or revised, should contain accurate information about provisions amending it or repealing (*the principle of self-closing*). This makes it possible to verify if the texts contain the current version of these regulations for the particular period of time and if particular regulations are properly numbered and organized into higher-order editorial units. This solution also allows for finding regulations that modify the particular text and to determine its earlier versions. Moreover, taking into account the above-mentioned sources of changes in the legal text, one can also determine whether electronic documents containing consolidated texts include changes introduced into the legal text, e.g. as a result of the decision of the Constitutional Tribunal. Another important principle is that of distinguishing the level of the content of the legal text and meta data describing the text (*the principle of distinguishing levels*). As a consequence, when the same event causes several changes to the document, all of them, if the need arises, will be properly classified and described both in a document containing the modified text, as well as in the modifying document. A similar situation applies to the distinguishing of the presentation layer of the document, which defines the form and style, in which the legal texts are published from the content layer of the document (*the principle of separating the presentation layer from the content of the document*).

The usability of the system of change management in the text of law depends largely on the level of the detailed specificity of the marked items. In fact, the system should identify each separate item included in the text of the law, and not just articles or sections, but also smaller editorial units, such as paragraphs, letters, indents, etc. (*the principle of granularity*). This makes it possible to achieve greater accuracy in data processing. At the same time,

[37] M. Palmirani, *Legislative Change Management with Akoma-Ntoso...*, p. 107.

the database of legal texts which manages the system should be complete, i.e. it should include all legal texts, described in markup languages, to allow the system for their adequate processing (*the principle of completeness*). It is a condition whose realization determines the ability to create consolidated versions of the texts, including any changes made by the legislator in the *system of sources of law*.

The text of the law is an extremely complex and dynamic network. As a result, a change in any of the items may interact with other items in the database. Therefore, to maintain the integrity of the whole system, it is necessary to create a mechanism for controlling the process of consolidation. The system, while creating a consolidated version, must take into account the entire network of formal relationships, which characterize consolidated texts by detecting anomalies in the relationships between the elements in the database, i.e. retroactive legislation, regulations entering into force later than the whole text of the act, in which they are contained or secondary legislation that is legally effective, despite the fact of repealing of legal force under which they were issued.

The last principle, which is worth mentioning, is *the principle of technological neutrality of standards used to build the system*. Technological neutrality in this context is to guarantee the ability to process data sets contained in the database in a way that shall be independent from the available technology, as a computing platform. Taking into consideration the stability of the legal system, automated change management system must be able to expand in accordance with the future needs of its potential users. As a result, the principles of its functioning must be sufficiently clear to allow for its future operation and development. Moreover, taking into account the needs of different groups of users, the system should provide access to data using any equipment that meets certain strictly defined and explicit terms.

6. Conclusions

While the promulgation of consolidated texts in the period of official journals which were published in print form undoubtedly facilitated the application of law, in the digital realm it will only increase the redundancy of legal information and may lead to completely unnecessary problems. Taking into consideration the fact that legal texts are currently prepared, stored and communicated in the form of electronic documents, the implementation of solutions discussed above makes it possible to retain the maximum consistency of information in the database of legal texts. Moreover, at the same time it allows for presentation of consolidated legal texts as of every moment, to each recipient, at any time, with the use of any device connected to the internet. The computerization of law allowed a clear distinction between the level of recording information and the level of information presentation.[38] As a result, it became technically possible to automatically generate and share a consolidated version of the legal text on the day selected by the user. The legal status of information which has been generated in such a way is, from the technical point of view, a secondary issue, because it is possible to present electronic documents containing legal texts in the form of a consolidated text, without having to create a separate electronic document with a consolidated text. Hence, there is no impediment to granting authenticity status to such a form of presentation provided, of course, that such consolidation will be done by a dedicated state system. Nevertheless, at least two conditions must be fulfilled, so that the system can be effective. First, electronic promulgation journals must be structured in such a way that allows for automation of the searching and management of information contained in them. Second, legal texts issued by all authorities which are entitled to do so must be created in accordance with the defined format of an electronic document, which not only enables unambiguous identification, accessibility on the Internet and the appropriate visualization, but also ensure that different computer systems exchanging information with each other will be able to properly interpret them.[39]

The operation of such a system through the use of information technology also allows for the viewing of the contents of electronic documents and additional information, influencing their normative level, without the need for the "physical" inclusion of such information in the content of these documents. This data can be made available in such a format to recipients through, for example, links. Thus it would be possible to increase the informativeness of texts which are made available to recipients with no violation of the integrity of the documents containing the legal text.

[38] To obtain more information please refer to W. Cyrul, J. Duda, J. Opiła, T. Pełech-Pilichowski, *Management of legal information in legal texts using markup languages*, in: P. Łebkowski (ed.), *Aspects of production engineering*, Kraków 2010, p. 65–95.

[39] See M. Tabor, *Standardization of electronic documents produced by public entities*, Electronic Administration, 2007, No. 5, p. 43 ff, www.cyfrowyurzad.pl (accessed 25.11.2013).

Chapter 6

A Three Dimensional – Code and a Question of the Normative Hyper-linking?

Fryderyk Zoll
Jagiellonian University in Kraków

1. A New Wave of Codifications – sometimes new content, but almost always old form

We are now experiencing in Europe a new wave of codifications.[1] Some of them are like a breath of fresh air; others merely develop or alter existing concepts. Appealing, however, is the reluctance to adopt new structures for the codes. The mode of the presentation of the legal matter remains mostly unaffected. Perhaps the most recent innovation in this field was (and this was more than 20 years ago) the new Dutch Civil Code. At least the system of numbering of the articles facilitates the development and the revisions of the text, albeit the quotation of the provisions is much more difficult. The system of the Dutch Civil Code is also interesting because it endorses a lot of the German tradition of the codification (one must remember that the starting point for the Dutch law is the French Code Civil), but it does not follow the pandectistic structure of the code.[2] Despite all of these innovations, since the pandectistic structure was developed and in reaction to it the anti-pandectis-

---

[1] R. Schulze, F. Zoll, *The Law of Obligations in Europe*, A New Wave of Codifitcations, Munich 2013.

[2] S. Grundmann, *The Architecture of European Codes and Contract Law – A Survey of Structures and Contents*, in: S. Grundmann, M. Schauer, *The Architecture of European Codes and Contract Law*, Alphen aan den Rijn 2006, p. 14–15.

tic codes (as a Swiss law)[3] drafted, nothing entirely new has happened which would revolutionize the structure of the codifications.

Whilst the use of technology has also changed the manner of usage of the legal texts immensely, it has not influenced the way in which texts are drafted. There is no structure of law which has developed with the express purpose of using new technology. The technological possibilities which have become available have not been taken into account in the process of drafting. The formal frames of the promulgation of the legal acts have not been changed, hence law-makers do not have a sufficient legal framework to experiment.

2. Academic drafts in the process of the Europeanization of the private law – PECL, DCFR, Gandolfi Draft – again, a rather conservative structure

The end of the 20th and the first decade of this century have been quite rich in terms of the various drafts pretending to restate the common European tradition, mostly of the contract law,[4] but also in the case of the DCFR which encompasses other fields of the private law.[5] In all these sources, the structure was not a field of experimentation and, for understandable reasons, they were more focused on the content. In case of the drafts related to the general contract law, the question of the structure was certainly not the primary concern. It was more complicated in case of the DCFR due to its scope, consisting of the big parts of the codification of the usual private law. The structure delivered by the DCFR is, however, also quite conservative. It also partially resembles a pandectistic structure,[6] even if it does not have a general part in the sense of the German Civil Code. It has not been drafted with the idea of being especially adjusted for electronic use.

---

[3] See on the Swiss Civil Code K. Zweigert, H. Kötz, *Einführung in die Rechtsvergleichung* (Introduction to the Comparative Law), Vol. 3, Tübingen 1996, p. 165–176.

[4] O. Lando, H. Beale, *Principles of European Contract Law*, Parts I and II, Hague 2000; O. Lando, E. Clive, A. Prüm, R. Zimmermann, *Principles of Contract Law*, Part III, Hague 2003; C. von Bar, E. Clive, *Draft Common Frame of Reference*, DCFR Full Edition, Munich 2009; U. Magnus, *European Law of Obligation*, Munich 2002; G. Gandolfi, *Code Europeen des Contrats*, Livre Deuxième 1, Milan 2007, and 2, Milan 2008; P. Catala, *Avant-projet de réforme du droit des obligations et de la prescription*, Paris 2006; B. Fauvarque-Cosson, D. Mazeaud, *Principes contractuels communs*, Paris 2008.

[5] About the DCFR see: H.-W. Micklitz, F. Cafaggi, *European Private Law after the Common Frame of Reference*, Cheltenham 2010.

[6] On the structure on the Draft Common Frame of Reference see C. von Bar, E. Clive, *DCFR*, Vol I. Introduction, p. Intr. 31–37; F. Zoll, *A Need for a New Structure for European Private Law*, in: R. Brownsword, H.-W. Micklitz, L. Niglia, S. Weatherhill, *The Foundations of European Private Law*, Oregon 2001, p. 557–558.

3. Structure of the existing acquis communautaire on the area of the contract law

European private law is characterized by the patchwork of the directives with the relatively narrow scope of application and different modus of the organization of the legal matter.[7] The structure of European private law was for a long time not really a matter of concern, due to the fact that the European acquis communautaire was not drafted as a coherent system of law, but rather envisaged as a completion of the national systems. The directives are however characterized by a "problem approach" to the legal matter.[8] A reader looking for a certain problem in the given life situation will find a set of rules applicable to this particular situation at one place. These rules are, however, often feasible for generalization and in the case of national law (if this national law is equipped with a code) they would be usually placed on the more abstract level. The approach of the Union's law – the "problem approach" facilitates the process of the understanding of the law, but it creates difficulties in the process of the implementation of the law into the national systems. From the perspective of the national system, it is usually impossible to maintain sufficient coherency of the system.[9]

The first decade of the 21st century has brought a change in the approach of the Union related to the question of the systematization of law.[10] The coherency of national law has been identified as a problem and the various communications of the Commission has formulated a program of achieving

[7] H. Schulte-Nölke, F. Zoll, *Structure and Values of the Principles: New features and their possible use for political puposes*, in: Research Group on the Existing EC Private Law (Acquis Group), *Principles of the Existing EC Contract Law (Acquis Pronciples) Contract II*, Munich 2009, p. xxiii–xxviii.

[8] H. Schulte-Nölke, F. Zoll, in: *Research Group on the Existing EC Private Law, Acquis Principles Contract II*, Munich 2009, p. xxv–xxvi.

[9] F. Zoll, *A need for a new structure of European Private Law*, in: R. Brownsword, H.-W. Micklitz et al., *The Foundations of European Private Law*, Oxford 2011, p. 559–560.

[10] Communication from the Commission to the European Parliament and the council, A more coherent European Contract Law – Action Plan, Brussels, 12.2.2003COM(2003) 68 final; Communication from the Commission to the European Parliament and the council, European Contract Law and the revision of the acquis: the way forward, Brussels, 11.10.2004 COM(2004) 651 final; Green Paper from the Commission on policy options for progress towards a European Contract Law for consumers and businesses, Brussels, 01.07.2010 COM(2010)348 final; Regarding the meaning of the Communication of the Commission COM(2003)68 final see: C. von Bar, E. Clive, *DCFR*, Vol I. Introduction, p. Intr. 50; G. Howells, R. Schulze, *Modernising and Harmonising Consumer Contract Law*, Munich 2009, Introduction; F. Zoll, *Der Entwurf des Gemeinsamen Referenzrahmens und die Vollharmonisierung*, in: M. Stürner, *Vollharmonisierung im Europäischen Verbraucherrecht*, Munich 2010, p. 133–141; F. Zoll, *A need for a new structure of European Private Law*, in: *The Foundations of European Private Law...*, p. 560–561.

a higher level of coherency of the acquis communautaire. One of the ideas was the so-called framework directive.[11] It has ended up in the new directive on consumer rights,[12] which in a very limited way brings some traces of the systematization of the consumer law.

Moreover, the Commission has formulated a proposal for the Common European Sales Law, an optional instrument.[13] This draft is unique for European legislation, because it contains a coherent, self-standing set of rules encompassing a broad field of the contractual relationship with the purpose of direct application. The structure of this instrument is a combination of general and specific parts. It is a quite traditional model, at the same time not entirely coherent.[14] The drafters have (probably rightly) not experimented with the structure, although they were – not always consistently – trying to combine the user friendly problem approach with the general pandectistic structure. Hence, the rules concerning non-performance are artificially narrowed down (with the exception of damages) and repeated in case separately for the seller, buyer, service provider and customer. Other rules, having the same content of generality, are regarded as common rules for all contracts covered by the instrument. There is a draft proposed by the European Law Institute suggesting a more coherent approach to the structure of the CESL. In all these cases, electronic technology has not been seen as a possible main environment for the drafts (which also results from the existing formal requirements for the sources of law).

---

[11] H. Schulte-Nölke, F. Zoll, in: *Research Group on the Existing EC Private Law, Acquis Principles Contract II*, p. xxv–xxvi; Green Paper from the Commission on policy options for progress towards a European Contract Law for consumers and businesses, Brussels, 01.07.2010 COM(2010)348 final.

[12] Directive 2011/83/EU of the European Parliament and of the Council of 25 October 2011 on consumer rights, amending Council Directive 93/13/EEC and Directive 1999/44/EC of the European Parliament and of the Council and repealing Council Directive 85/577/EEC and Directive 97/7/EC of the European Parliament and of the Council, Official Journal of the European Union of 22.11.2011, L 304/64.

[13] Proposal for a Regulation of the European Parliament and of the Council on a Common European Sales Law, Brussels, 11.10.2011 COM(2011) 635 final 2011/0284 (COD); R. Schulze, Commentary on *Common European Sales Law (CESL)*, Baden-Baden 2012.

[14] H. Schulte-Nölke, *Scope and Function of the Optional Instrument on European Contract Law*, in: R. Schulze, J. Stuyck, *Towards a European Contract Law*, Munich 2011, p. 39–40. About the dogmatics, the methodology and structure of the Common European Sales Law see: C. Herresthal, *Zur Dogmatik und Methodik des Gemeinsamen Europöischen Kaufrechts nach dem Vorschlag der Kaufrechts-Verordnung*, in: H. Schulte-Nölke, F. Zoll, N. Jansen, R. Schulze, *Der Entwurf für ein optionales europäisches Kaufrecht*, Munich 2012, p. 88–106; On the Common European Sales Law see: M. Schmidt-Kessel, *Ein einheitliches europäisches Kaufrecht?*, Munich 2012.

4. The Acquis Principles

The Acquis Principles are probably the only text of all various European academic drafts which have been envisaged to also have in mind the technological possibility of presenting the legal text. Even this text was never presented in this way and its probable feasibility for the usage of new technologic platforms has never been tried, a perspective of the use of the technology has also been seen while drafting the structure of the Acquis Principles.[15] Hence, they are constructed in a way which tries to combine the problem approach of the directives with the new-pandectistic generalization. The structure of the Acquis Principles has been described in various places[16] and probably there is no need to do it in detail once again. I would therefore like to focus only on the issues which could be relevant from the perspective of their feasibility for the new technology for presenting a legal matter.

The Acquis Principles have been drafted in order to restate the European law spread through the numerous directives and other sources. Their purpose was to present the existing contract law of the EU as already a system, capable of governing contractual relationships. As I mentioned above, the European contract law is not constructed as a system, but it already has elements which – if one were to put them together, generalize them and sometimes fill the gaps – depicted an almost full-fledged contract law. By collecting and arranging the acquis communautaire on contracts, the drafters of this group were trying to combine two underlining principles of contract law which were in certain contradiction to each other: the problem approach of the directive, which also enables people without any background in law to understand or at least to have an impression of understanding of the legal text and the principle of generalization of rules, which are feasible for such generalization, which means that they can apply to other factual patterns as well, as those covered by the directive's scope of application. These two approaches are very difficult to reconcile, if only using them in two dimensional environments. However, the Acquis-Group has tried to find a way to unify these two approaches. Hence, the so called a "mirror structure"[17] has been invented. This mirror structure exists of numerous small general parts, e.g. on pre-contractual duties, formation of contract, unfair terms, performance and non-performance, etc. The small particular parts are added to each gene-

---

[15] F. Zoll, *A need for a new structure of European Private Law*, in: R. Brownsword, H.-W. Micklitz et al., *The Foundations of European Private Law...*, p. 555–561.

[16] C. von Bar, E. Clive, *DCFR*, Vol I. *Introduction...*, p. Intr. 31–37; F. Zoll, *A need for a new structure of European Private Law*, in: R. Brownsword, H.-W. Micklitz et al., *The Foundations of European Private Law...*, p. 557–558.

[17] F. Zoll, *A need for a new structure of European Private Law*, in: R. Brownsword, H.-W. Micklitz et al., *The Foundations of European Private Law...*, p. 559–560.

ral part, containing rules which are only applicable to specific situations like package travel, time sharing, distance contract, etc. It means that the particular rules on package travel appear in different places – not in one piece of legislation, but scattered through the text, linked to the small "general parts" so far as they modify them. The user of the text looking for the solution applicable in a non-performance situation will find particular and also general rules in one place. It is probably easier as in the usual pandectistic structure, where the non-performance provisions will appear in different places, since linking them usually requires a high level of competence.

The structure of the Acquis Principles allows the retention of certain advantages of the problem approach, but equally provides a system applicable to a range of situations, not directly covered by the particular rules. It may fulfil the function of national contract law, but is very strongly based on the values reflected by the acquis communautaire. The structure as used in the two-dimensional environment, however, cannot prove all advantages it possess. The user would find a set of rules in one place, related to package travel, belonging to a different level of generality, but still this user would face difficulties in linking this part of the text to other parts. The Acquis Principles may prove their full functionality only if displayed in three dimensions.

5. Acquis Principles in 3D

The "mirror structure" used in the three dimensions may facilitate further the usage of the text.[18] The use of technology would facilitate the operation on the text even at the simplest level. As I have discussed above, the particular rules (e.g. on non-performance in package travel) are linked with the general rules on non-performance. In practice, it is not so easy to link the particular with the general rules, due to the fact that the Acquis Principles have to deal with numerous situations, like payment services, consumer credits, independent agents, delayed payments, etc. A user does not see its particular rules on package travels directly below the general rules on non-performance. The use of technology would make it possible to display the rules, which cannot be seen in the text at one place as a coherent set of rules. By making a hyperlink it would be possible. Having a general rule, the user would find the links to the particular situation just below the general rule. By clicking on the rules of package travel, the main rule and the package-travel specific exception would be displayed in one connected portion.

---

[18] H. Schulte-Nölke, F. Zoll, *Research Group on the Existing EC Private Law, Acquis Principles Contract II...*, p. xxv–xxvi.

This hyperlinking would allow one to go even further in a such situation and connect the rules, belonging to the different part of the text. A person starting from a rule on damages could also click on rules on formation of the contract, on the right to withdraw and on the rule governing the content of performance. In this way, all of the relevant rules would be presented in one place, allowing the particular user to benefit from the problem approach, while the whole structure would remain its general feature as the codification encompassing a broad spectrum of legal relationships.

6. The normativity of the hyperlinking

Is it imaginable to have a code, where the hyperlinking between the different parts of this code would be also accepted as a normative expression of the law-maker?[19] In such a code the different parts would be connected with each that a person seeking an answer to the real problem of law would be able to display at one place a set of rules applicable to this particular problem. In such system trough the links the rule will obtain additional normative content through the links, because this link would also show with which rules located in the other part of law this one is especially connected. The code would get an additional dimension, because the system of references would allow the gathering of most of the relevant provisions applicable in the given case in one place. It would mean, however, that the existence of a hyperlink would be treated as a part of the norm – another sort of a legal reference. Of course, it could not exclude the necessity to also find another connection among the rules, beyond the system of the hyperlinks, but at least the most typical situations would be covered by such system. In that case the law would be better to adjust to the factual pattern and probably easier in application. A person looking for the answer of whether the bequeather could testate would connect the rule on capability to testate with the general rules governing the legal capacity of the physical persons and would get the complete set of the rules displayed at one place applicable to the given situation. It would require better coordination between different parts of the code, because a legislator would be forced to examine numerous connections, whether they create a reasonable body of law.

In the case of the Acquis Principles, a certain structure has been developed in which it will be easier to examine whether such hyperlinked code

[19] See also: F. Zoll, *Das Pandektensystem und die Vorschriften über den Vertragsschluss in der Struktur des polnischen Zivilgesetzbuches*, in: Ch. Baldus, W. Dajczak, *Der Allgemeine Teil des Privatrechts. Erfahrungen zwischen Deutschland, Polen und lusitanischen Rechten*, Frankfurt am Main 2013, p. 136–137.

could really work. One has to venture to prepare the software presented in this text in such an environment which would allow experimentation in the application of the law this way. Perhaps it is a path for the codification in the future which would be drafted to be displayed only electronically and only in the electronic environment would a rule get its full meaning.

Chapter 7

The Law, Labour Unions and Information Technology: Enhancing or Restricting Democracy at the Workplace

Laura Carlson
Stockholm University

1. Introduction

The use of information technology within the law is typically seen as the process of capturing and digitalizing legal decisions for easy dissemination, for example through databases. However, information technology can also be seen as affecting the actual law-making process. This arguably is the case with the use by the labour unions in Sweden with respect to information technology and social media in the collective bargaining process. Due to the uniqueness of the Swedish labour law model, this use can be seen as directly affect the making of the law, here collective agreements. The use of information technology within this setting raises the question of whether democracy in the workplace is enhanced or restricted. This article first sets out the parameters of the Swedish labour law model, and then looks at the relationship of the social partners and their members. The third section takes up the use of social media and information technology by certain of the Swedish social partners. The article concludes with a discussion whether this use moves the law forward, or instead, leaves the law-making simply in the hands of those who are most technically savvy, in essence diminishing democracy in the work place as opposed to expanding it.

2. The Swedish labour law model

The Swedish labour law model (*den svenska arbetsrättsmodellen*), established already at the turn of the twentieth century, is characterized by a high degree of self-regulation between the social partners. It falls within the "Nordic labour law model",[1] perceived of as a third alternative to the more liberal, deregulated models found in countries such as the United Kingdom, and the more regulated models such as in Germany. Labour law (collective labour law) has historically been the primary focus of efforts between the social partners in the form of collective agreements as well as that of the statutory regulation. Employment law (individual labour law) has only fairly recently come more into focus, and arguably mostly due to the requirements of EU membership beginning in the 1990's, when Sweden became a member in 1995. Little employment legislation existed prior to EU membership, with the majority of such legislation now in place as a direct effect of EU membership.

2.1. The historical origins of the Swedish labour law model

Sweden went from being one of the last agricultural societies in Europe to industrialization in record time, basically an approximately thirty year time span, from 1860 to 1890. The dismantling of the guild system in the 1850's and 1860's led to an immediate organizational density among both employers and employees, one of the highest in Europe already by the 1900's. Sweden's historical context, combined with the fact that the social partners in the Swedish labour market have had little organisational segmentation, has allowed for the creation and duration of large and powerful umbrella and central organisations, as well as national trade based associations, on both the employer and employee sides. Founded in 1898, Landsorganisation i Sverige (LO)[2] is the strongest employee organisation in Sweden. The first two national central employer organisations were founded already in 1902, the Swedish Metal Trades Employers' Associa-

---

[1] In general, the Nordic legal model is seen as half-way between common law and civil law legal traditions. There has never been a codification of all laws in Sweden (the last code, drafted in 1736, was a compilation of existing laws), while at the same time certain areas of law rely heavily on case law. The Swedish legislative technique has been to enact fairly general laws with little detail. The court then turns to the legislative preparatory works when interpreting the laws to help fill in the lack of detail. This lack of detail in labour and employment law is supplied instead by the collective agreements first, then the legislative preparatory works.

[2] LO currently covers 1.5 million of the 4.7 million employees (2012, www.scb.se, accessed 25.11.2013) in the Swedish labour market. For more information in English on this central organization, see its website at www.lo.se (accessed 25.11.2013).

tion[3] and the Swedish Employers' Confederation, the latter the forerunner to the current Confederation of Swedish Enterprise.[4] The "December Compromise" was reached between these three umbrella organisations in 1906. The bi-partite pattern of the central organisations resolving labour market conflicts and establishing rights and duties without state involvement was laid, largely unchanged to the present day with the exceptions made due to EU law requirements. Much of the strength of this model has also depended upon the political situation in Sweden, with the Social Democrats the majority power almost without interruption from the 1930's until the past decade.

The central organisations on the employer and private employee sides entered into the Basic Agreement in 1938, also known as the Saltsjöbads Agreement, which is still in effect today, reinforcing the Swedish model of cooperation between the social partners, the employer and employee central organisations, and the state's expressed policy of neutrality to labour issues.[5] Five main topics were covered in the Basic Agreement: A Labour Market Council was established, which through mutual appointments to the Council, the central organisations would deal with specific labour market issues. Second, a negotiation procedure was established between the parties as to handling labour disputes. Third, employers conceded the right to freely terminate and/or lay-off employees, agreeing instead to a procedure by which the union would be notified in such cases, and if the parties were unable to resolve the issue, the matter would be referred to the Council. The counterbalance to this concession by the employers was the fourth point in the agreement, limiting the rights of employees to take industrial actions in certain contexts, such as cases of retaliation or potential damages to third parties, proscribing a duty to maintain industrial peace. Finally, the parties agreed that industrial actions that could potentially disrupt vital public interests were to be assessed by the Council for any threats posed. If these threats were

[3] The Swedish Metal Trades Employers' Association, Sveriges verkstadsförening, which in 1991 became part of the Swedish Metalworking Industries' Association, Sveriges verkstadsindustrier, renamed as of May 2003 to Association of Swedish Engineering Industries, Teknikföretagen. For more information in English on this latter organization, see its website at www.teknikforetagen.se (accessed 25.11.2013).

[4] The Swedish Employers' Confederation, Svenska Arbetsgivareföreningen (SAF). SAF joined with the Federation of Swedish Industries, Industriförbundet, in 2001 to become the Confederation of Swedish Enterprise, Svenska Näringsliv. For more information in English on the latter organization, see its website at www.svensktnaringsliv.se (accessed 25.11.2013).

[5] Negotiations between the Confederation of Swedish Enterprises, the Swedish Trade Union Confederation (LO) and the Council for Negotiation and Cooperation (PTK) on a new Basic Agreement for the private sector were held in 2008 with the aim of reaching a new Basic Agreement by the current one's 70th anniversary. Negotiations broke down by 2009 as the Confederation of Swedish Enterprises decided there was no further point in continuing. The lack of agreement was deemed to concern primarily two areas: the regulations regarding industrial disputes and selection order in the event of dismissals due to redundancy.

deemed too great, the industrial action was to be enjoined by the Council. The State during this period up until the 1970's refrained to a great extent from statutory regulation of the relationships on the labour market, permitting the social partners to regulate these matters instead through the above agreement and other collective agreements.

A statutory distinction is made between private and public employees, with the later regulated under the 1994 Public Employment Act. The private sector is further divided (informally by labour market organizations, not by law) between white and blue-collar workers, and the public sector between state and municipal/county council employees. Two-thirds of all employees are employed in the private sector. The public sector is large: nearly 35% of all employees work for the state or local authorities, and of these 35%, two-thirds are women. As a result of the extensive changes in the laws governing employment in the public sector, introduced successively in 1965, 1976 and 1994, wages and other conditions and terms of employment for state and municipal employees are now mainly regulated by collective agreements. Certain matters still cannot be regulated by collective agreement on account of the special regulations as found primarily in the 1994 Public Employment Act, and in a special agreement from 1976 for the public sector, but these exceptions are not particularly extensive.

2.2. Swedish labour legislation

The hierarchy of legal sources within Swedish labour and employment law can generally be seen as:

- Constitutional Rights and Protections (Freedom of speech, association, right to take industrial action).[6]
- Fundamental Rights (as found in the European Convention[7] or required by EU law).
- Mandatory Statutory Rights (cannot be derogated from by the social partners through a collective agreement, more the exception than the rule, and mostly as adopted due to Union law requirements).

---

[6] As regards international public law generally, Sweden has adopted the dualistic, rather than monistic, principle, entailing that international conventions must be enacted as Swedish law in order to be given effect as national law. When Sweden has ratified an international convention involving labour law norms without enacting the convention as national law, the ratification is considered to create a presumption that current national law is in conformance with the convention's norms. However, individuals cannot assert the rights, only states, under any international instrument not yet enacted as Swedish law.

[7] The European Convention of 1950 on the Protection of Human Rights and Fundamental Freedoms ("European Convention"), ratified by Sweden in 1950, was adopted as Swedish law in the form of the Swedish Human Rights Act in 1994, effective as law in 1998, see SFS 1994:1219.

- Collective Agreements.
- Statutory rights in the absence of a collective agreement.
- Case law.
- Good labour market practices.
- Individual Employee Agreements.
- Individual Employer Practices.
- Legal Scholarship.

The majority of the labour and employment law legislation in effect today can be traced either to a legislative packet enacted in the 1970's (and since amended) when labour had the upper hand due to a shortage of workers or to EU membership. The 1970 legislative packet began with a new constitutional act as adopted in 1974, the Instrument of Government, creating constitutional protections for freedom of expression as well as for freedom of association and the freedom to take industrial action.[8] The Employment Protection Act,[9] the Trade Union Representative (Status at the Workplace) Act,[10] the Employee's Right to Educational Leave Act,[11] as well as the Labour Disputes (Judicial Procedure) Act,[12] were passed in 1974. The Joint Regulation Act,[13] as well as the Act on the Right to Parental Leave,[14] were passed in 1976. A new Vacation Act,[15] as well as the Work Environment Act, were passed in 1977. The first Equal Treatment between Women and Men in Employment Act[16] was passed in 1979. One of the most permeating features of all of this legislation is that the social partners were given the right to contract out of the legislation through central agreements, even with respect to the constitutional provision concerning the protection of the right to take industrial action.

Labour law, the law governing collective agreements and the social partners as well as their relationship, has a predominantly private law character in Sweden. A characteristic feature of Swedish labour law is the emphasis on the role of the labour market organisations, the social partners, in the administration of collective agreements and legislation. These organisations generally

---

[8] An English translation of the Instrument of Government is available at the website of the Swedish Parliament, see www.riksdagen.se (accessed 25.11.2013).

[9] SFS 1974:12 replaced by SFS 1982:80.

[10] SFS 1974:358.

[11] SFS 1974:981.

[12] SFS 1974:371.

[13] SFS 1976:580. This Act has also been translated with the title, Employment (Co-Determination in the Workplace) Act. For an English translation of this act, and other labour legislation, see the website of the Government Offices of Sweden at www.government.se (accessed 25.11.2013).

[14] SFS 1976:280, replaced already in 1978 by SFS 1978:410.

[15] SFS 1977:480.

[16] SFS 1979:503 and then SFS 1979:1118.

have the right to institute judicial proceedings on behalf of their members in labour disputes. Trade unions are in essence responsible on behalf of their members for the supervision of the application of collective agreements, as well as general legislation and other rules. The regulations concerning information, consultation and other forms of employee control in the sphere of company management, is also considered part of labour law in Sweden as normally, it is the unions bound by collective agreements that act as holders of the rights of employees in such matters. Collective agreements between the parties are regulated only to a certain extent by law, as are individual employment agreements. In the absence of explicit legislation and collective agreements, the Court turns to general contract law and other private law for solutions.

2.3. Collective agreements

There are few statutory requirements as to collective agreements with the social partners having fairly extensive freedom with respect to their content. In accordance with Section 23 of the Joint Regulation Act, a collective agreement is to be a written agreement that concerns employment terms and conditions or the relationship in general between employees and the employer. The primary issues taken up in collective agreements are wages and employment terms and conditions.[17] Work environment, employment leave and travel compensation are examples of issues that can also be taken up, but nothing further is explicitly stated in the statute as to that which is required of the content of the collective agreements. The Swedish Labour Court has held, however, that the social partners do not have the right to negotiate with respect to already vested employment benefits, in essence that the social partners cannot retroactively negotiate vested employee rights, unless explicit consent to this has been given by the employees.[18]

Collective agreements fall into four main categories by sector: public sector state, public sector municipalities and county councils, private sector salaried employees and private sector blue-collar workers. One employer can be bound by several collective agreements regarding its workforce, for example,

---

[17] In addition to the collective agreements, individual employment contracts (a rather recent phenomenon) can be entered into between employers and individual employees. The terms of these differ considerably depending upon the labour market sector. The main requirement as to an individual employment contract is that it may not be in conflict with the prevalent collective agreement. The individual employment agreements are also generally governed by private law contract regulations.

[18] See for example AD 1947 No. 13 and AD 1958 No. 23(2). *Arbetsdomstolens domar* (AD) is the series in which the judgments of the Swedish Labour Court are published, by year of decision and order of judgment. The judgments of the Swedish Labour Court starting from 2003 are available on-line at the website of the Labour Court, www.arbetsdomstolen.se (accessed 25.11.2013).

with respect to salaried employees and blue-collar workers. Collective agreements can also exist on three levels, local, national and central. The agreements can overlap both horizontally and vertically. Certain central agreements as adopted by the umbrella organisations, such as LO, PTK, SACO or the Confederation of Swedish Enterprise, recommended agreements, must be adopted by the national organisations to be applicable. Local agreements can also be entered into between local labour unions and employers, but these are effective only at that work place. Employers not already members of an employer organisation can be given the option of signing an already existing collective agreement, an accessory or tie-in agreement (*hängavtal*), usually containing a minimum of terms and conditions mirroring those found in the collective agreement for the sector.

Certain national agreements as adopted by LO, TCO or SACO, recommended agreements, must be adopted by the individual labour unions to become applicable. Local agreements can also be entered into between labour unions and the employer, but these are only effective locally, in other words, at the local work place. No statutory requirement exists that each work place must have a collective agreement. However, the Joint Regulation Act grants labour unions means for inducing employers to sign collective agreements, namely through industrial action. The duty to maintain the industrial peace does not exist in the absence of a collective agreement.

Collective agreements are legally binding on both parties to the agreement, as well as on the members of the organisations that have reached such agreements. There is however no *ergo omnes* affect given to collective agreements. An employer and employee bound by a collective agreement cannot enter into a separate agreement that is not consistent with the terms of the collective agreement, unless the latter permits such derogation. Thus collective agreements have a mandatory effect on individual agreements. A breach of a collective agreement entails a liability for damages to the injured party, even if no economic loss has been suffered. The law does not specify any upper limit of such exemplary damages, but normally the judgment awards by the Swedish Labour Court are fairly modest.

Collective agreements are to be re-negotiated prior to their expiration. There are some 60 unions and about 50 employer bodies, in all, there are over a hundred contracting parties in the Swedish labour market, reaching over 650 collective agreements covering approximately 3.6 million employees.[19] During 2013 over 500 collective agreements covering roughly 3.3 million Swedish workers, will be renegotiated. One of the major issues during

---

[19] For these statistics and others as to collective agreements, see the website of the Swedish governmental agency charged with mediating disputes in the Swedish labour market, Medlingsinstitutet, at www.mi.se (accessed 25.11.2013). This agency is to receive an archival copy of each collective agreement reached.

negotiations is wage setting. No minimum wage legislation exists in Sweden. The social partners regulate wage-setting instead through collective agreements. Another characteristic feature of the relationships on the Swedish labour market is that collective agreements on wages and general terms of employment are normally reached centrally, for entire business sectors for the entire country. A national agreement is usually reached for an entire business sector, and thereafter supplemented by local agreements. It is nowadays common, particularly in the state sector, that wage increases decided on the central level are distributed to individual employees through decisions taken entirely at the local level.

2.4. Entering into a collective agreement

A general right to negotiate was recognized at the turn of the twentieth century in the collective agreements, and first explicitly recognized by statute in the 1936 Act on the Right to Organise and Negotiate. This protection was retained in the Joint Regulation Act. Section 10 of the act defines the right as belonging to an employee organisation "to negotiate with an employer on any matter relating to the relationship between the employer and any member of the organisation who is, or has been, employed by that employer".

If an employee organisation approaches an employer with the objective of reaching a collective agreement, the employer must attend the negotiations and discuss the demands presented, a duty sanctioned under the act by damages. Such an obligation to negotiate exists even if the union only has one member at the workplace. The general right to negotiate as granted by Section 10 of the Joint Regulation Act does not create any obligation on the part of either party to reach an agreement.

If the parties cannot come to an agreement, and there is no collective agreement already in place between the parties, the social partners are normally free to take industrial action, a right protected by Article 14 of chapter two of the Instrument of Government. Such conflicts are termed "interest disputes" for which industrial action is an appropriate resolution mechanism. Industrial action can take the form of a strike, lockout or boycott or any similar measure against the other party, failing any provision to the contrary by law. Industrial action is not defined by statute, but rather purposively untouched to allow for greater flexibility and protection of rights. The National Mediation Office is currently empowered under the Act to attempt to resolve industrial disputes through mediation. Other restrictions as regards the right to industrial action exist in certain basic agreements concluded centrally. The Parliament is empowered under the Instrument of Government to intervene statutorily in certain cases. The Government, however, cannot act solely in such issues.

As soon as a collective agreement is reached, the right of the parties to take industrial action in principle ceases according to Sections 41–42 of the Joint Regulation Act. Industrial action may not be taken in order to bring about changes in a collective agreement. Such a conflict with respect to amending a collective agreement is termed a "rights dispute" and must first be negotiated and failing a resolution by the parties, ultimately taken to the Labour Court instead. Settlements in such cases are quite common, as the social partners prefer to resolve their disputes internally rather than judicially. A party to a collective agreement, however, is generally entitled to take secondary actions (*sympatiåtgärder*) without restrictions in order to assist another party in an on-going lawful labour conflict.

A social partner that has taken an unlawful industrial action can be sanctioned by the Labour Court in the form of damages. On the labour side, only the labour unions can exercise the right to take industrial action. An employee may not take industrial action without the sanction of the respective labour union. If unlawful, liability for damages caused by the action may be imposed on individual employees, though normally not in an amount exceeding SEK 2 000 per employee. In the event an organisation has organised the unlawful action, individual employees cannot be sanctioned by damages for participation in the action.

2.5. The Swedish system of joint regulation (co-determination)

Once a collective agreement has been entered into between the social partners, it can be seen as further cemented by the system of joint regulation created through the combination of legislation and self-regulation by the social partners as described above. Joint regulation had existed between the social partners through agreement before the enactment of the 1970's legislation, but then became affixed by statute. The Swedish model of joint regulation differs from the German model of works councils. However, in line with the requirements of Union law, Sweden has adopted the necessary legislation with respect to works councils for European companies.

The employer has the right to freely direct and allocate work unless otherwise provided by statute or relevant agreement. As the employers' freedoms with respect to employment were curtailed, the rights of employees through labour unions to influence the employer's decision-making processes at different levels were expanded. All labour market organisations have the rights concerning freedom of association and the general right to negotiate as discussed above. However, special rights are granted to the labour union that has succeeded first in reaching a collective agreement with an employer. This union is then deemed the "established" or signatory union. The Joint Regulation Act guarantees special rights to established unions in that they become representatives of the interests of the entire workforce at a given work place in all significant matters concerning joint regulation.

The current statutory regulations concerning joint regulation are primarily those as set out in the Joint Regulation Act and other acts as discussed below. The structure of joint regulation and labour union influence can be seen to comprise the following:

- Statutory rights for labour union representatives, including paid time--off to conduct union activities.
- The primary right to negotiate and the employer's duty to consult with the labour unions.
- The labour union's right to information.
- The union's right to veto certain employer decisions.
- The right of interpretation by the union with respect to certain issues under the collective agreements such as the employee's duty to perform work.
- The establishment and rights of employee safety delegates at the work place; and
- Mandatory representation of employees on the board of directors for private corporations and public entities.

Many of these statutory provisions concerning joint regulation are quasi-mandatory, entailing that the social partners are free to contract out of them with the exception of those rights provided to employees under EU law. Section 32 of the Joint Regulation Act encourages the parties to a collective agreement regulating wages and similar matters to enter into an agreement about entering into agreements. Upon the request of the employee party, the parties are also to negotiate a collective agreement concerning the employees' right to joint regulation.

3. The social partners, members and collective agreements

swedish employees historically have been highly organised, with highs of over 85% of trade union membership, a figure fairly consistent since the beginning of the twentieth century. Union membership exists even at the highest professional levels, such for judges and physicians. A contributing factor to this very high degree of organisation, when compared internationally, can be seen as the fact that many social benefits, such as unemployment and sickness benefits, historically were administered by the unions. The Swedish state assumed complete responsibility for the sick pay system in the 1960's, and reduced state subsidies to the union unemployment funds in 2006. After the reduction in 2006 union member density in the blue-collar sector has dropped to 68% and in the white-collar, 73% (2012)[20] attributed in part to the fact that the costs of the unemployment insurance as no longer state subsidized were passed onto the union members. At the time of this writing, the degree of membership density among employers is higher at 90% than among employees.

The internal affairs of labour market organisations in general are not regulated by law. Section 11 of Chapter Two of the 2008 Discrimination Act expressly prohibits unlawful discrimination on the basis of sex, transgender identity or expression, ethnicity, religion or other belief, disability, sexual orientation or age within employee and employer organisations with respect to membership, benefits as well as participation in activities. Otherwise, each labour market organisation regulates matters internally through its own organisational bylaws.

There are no statutory requirements with respect to creating a labour organization in Sweden, with Section 6 of the Joint Regulation Act simply stating:

> SECTION 6 By employee organisation is meant such an association of employees that pursuant to its by-laws is charged with safeguarding the interests of employees in relation to the employer. By employer organisation is meant an equivalent association of employers.
>
> By local employee organisation is meant an association of employees that is a party to local negotiations with an employer. By central employee organisation is meant a national or equivalent association of employees.
>
> The provisions relating to employer organisations or employee organisations shall apply, where relevant, to an association of several such organisations. In such cases, that which is said as to members in an organisation shall apply to the member organisations and their members.

There is no legal requirement as to representing employees. Consistent with the self-regulation model, the social partners have been very free to decide these issues. However, if an organization assumes a legally recognized form, such as a corporation or limited partnership, it needs to follow the general statutory requirements for that legal form. However, again, there are no statutory requirements as to representation. The social partners are represented by strong centralized organisations on both sides, each having a hierarchy comprising of umbrella organisations, central national labour or employee unions belonging to the umbrella organisations, then local and club organisations belonging to the central national unions. National central

[20] See Statistics Sweden at www.scb.se (accessed 25.11.2013).

collective agreements are entered into between the social partners, however, the agreements are adopted on the member level within these organisations.

3.1. The organizational structure of the social partners

In Sweden there are central umbrella organizations on both the employee and employers sides. Affiliated with each of these are national associations, which in their turn can have affiliates in the form of local employers, unions and clubs.

Employer side

Within the public sector, the umbrella employer organisations are the Swedish Agency for Government Employers for the state, covering 250 employer members having 240 000 employees, and the Swedish Association of Local Authorities and Regions (SALAR) for the municipalities and county councils, covering employer members with approximately 900 000 employees. On the private employer side, the main organisation is the Confederation of Swedish Enterprise. It has 50 sector and employer organizations representing more than with 54 000 member companies having together almost 1.5 million employees. The Confederation of Swedish Enterprise does not negotiate wages. These three umbrella organisations together cover almost 2.7 million employees. There are also several smaller private employer organisations, such as the Banking Sector Employers Organisation with 150 member banks having 45 000 employees, and KFO with commercial cooperatives as members, including 2 300 such organisations with 85 000 employees.

Employee side

LO, TCO and SACO are the major central organisations on the employee side. The Swedish Trade Union Confederation (LO, www.lo.se, accessed 25.11.2013) is the umbrella organisation covering mainly blue-collar workers, 80 per cent of all industrial workers and 60 per cent of blue-collar workers in the service sector. With its 14 national unions having nearly 1.5 million members, it is the largest employee organisation. In the salaried employee sector, the Confederation of Professional Employees (TCO, www.tco.se, accessed 25.11.2013) is the largest organisation with 15 affiliated national unions and approximately 1.2 million members. The Swedish Confederation of Professional Associations (SACO, www.saco.se, accessed 25.11.2013) mainly organizes university-educated employees, with 22 affiliated national unions and having approximately 630 000 members. Apart from these three well-established umbrella organisations, there are only a few smaller organisations.

It is unusual for trade unions to compete as to organising the same groups of employees. In addition to these umbrella organizations is the syndicalist Central Organization of Sweden's Workers (SAC). In 2009 SAC was responsible for over 65 per cent of all notices of industrial action served in Sweden, none of which concerned disputes as to wages or general terms of employment.

That the national unions belong to different national federations does not prevent them from collaborating in negotiating cartels or coalitions as against a certain counter party. One example in the private sector is the Federation of Salaried Employees in Industry and Services (PTK, www.ptk.se, accessed 25.11.2013), comprising 26 national unions from TCO and SACO representing 700 000 employees. PTK negotiates with the Confederation of Swedish Enterprise on pensions and insurance. Fourteen national unions in the public sector from both SACO and TCO collaborate in the Public Employees' Negotiation Council (OFR, www.ofr.se, accessed 25.11.2013), representing about 560 000 regional and local government employees. In March 1997, the negotiating parties in Swedish industry – 12 employer organisations and 7 trade unions – reached a collaboration agreement on industrial development and wage formation, covering approximately 600 000 employees from such unions as the Association of Graduate Engineers, the IF Metall (for metal-workers and industrial workers) and Unionen (for white-collar workers).

In addition, most employment market organizations are structured to have several contact points with the outside world, not just as between employers and employees. For example, a labour union has its relationship to the national union organisation and to other closely-related unions in the sector, on the national level, the European level and the international level. There can be contacts generally between these, but also networks created concerning specific issues such as legal issues, equality, work environment, the labour market sector, occupational injuries, social insurance, and traffic injuries, as is the case with the Teachers' Union. Other topics involving both unions, employer organizations and the state can be proposed legislation, statistics, pension and insurance issues, negotiation processes, etc. The Teacher's Union has over 60 areas in which different constellations of unions, employer organizations and state bodies interact.

3.2. The social partners and their members

The bylaws of the labour market organisations define the mutual rights and duties between the members and the organisations. There is no Swedish legislation explicitly regulating the internal affairs of labour market organisations. However, the 2008 Discrimination Act expressly prohibits unlawful discrimination by employee and employer organisations on the basis of sex, transgender identity or expression, ethnicity, religion or other belief, disability, sexual orientation or age with respect to employment, labour market policy, professional recognition and membership in organisations. There is no general duty of representation by labour unions as to its members other than as set out in the union's bylaws and in contract law under the rules governing principals and agents. The Swedish legal model in labour law is based on the fundamental premise that those areas not covered by the labour law legislation or by collective agreements will be regulated by general private law, mostly general contract law as well as agency law. As there is no *ergo omnes*, public law does not touch upon issues of representation or of collective agreements. There is no distinction here with respect to the treatment of union representation and general agency under private and public law.

Governance and consequently representation within the labour unions is handled primarily on two levels, as typically set out in the labour union's bylaws, a national level and a local level. These two levels can also have different tiers. On the national level, there are the congresses and the boards of the labour unions, the latter often also supported by other bodies. On the local level, there can be a local club at a workplace or for a specific professional group of employees, as well as regional clubs and interest organisations. Another key element on the local level is the contact ombudsperson. The constellation of the different tiers within the two levels can vary from union to union, but the majority is organised around these two levels.

As to the labour union bylaws setting out issues of authority, representation and governance, these typically are adopted and amended by the labour union's congress. There is no one universal model for such bylaws. One example that can be named here is the bylaws of the Teachers' Labour Union (Lärarförbundet). The bylaws, as adopted by the 2010 Congress, begin first by stating the general principles as held by the union, that the Teachers' Union is a labour union for teachers, school leaders and student teachers, and that it is to ensure the interests of its members. The bylaws then set out the overarching values of the labour union with respect to human rights, equality, solidarity, international cooperation, political non-partisanship and democracy. Under the subsection democracy, the bylaws state that the labour union's objective is to ensure the needs and contribute to solving the problems of its members, solutions which may not always be attainable on the individual level for everyone. That section continues by stating that

> in order to be successful, our demands must be understood as legitimate and rest upon the efforts of many, active and united members. The decisions by the Teachers' Union as well as the direction of the focus of its work, is to be formed in part at the workplace and at the members of the meetings, where all members are to have a say, and also partly through representatives who are appointed democratically by the majority.

This section ends with the statement that democracy is a requisite in order for the Teachers' Union to be a strong labour union, consequently all operations in the union are to be conducted and organised in a manner that best supports the democratic process.

The bylaws of the Teachers' Union also state the union's objectives:

- To improve the conditions for individuals and the collective as well as strengthen the influence over and conditions for the profession of teaching.
- Develop and strengthen the teaching profession.
- Develop and strengthen the professional development of teachers.
- Strive for the development of teaching academically; and
- Influence societal development in issues that are important for students, teachers and the schools.

Included among the member's rights is the right to take up issues as member meetings and motions to the Congresses.

Another example of bylaws that can be mentioned in this context are the bylaws of the union representing employees (as well as the self-employed) in the finance sector (Finansförbundet). These bylaws also begin with general principles, such as being based on the values characterizing a democratic rule of law country, as expressed by the Swedish constitution, the UN Charter of Human Rights, as well as the European Convention. The second principle cited is that the union is to closely guard both the right of association as well as the right to negotiate. The third principle is that the union is to cooperation with Swedish, Nordic and international organisations addressing the same issues.

Instead of taking up the issue of negotiation under the different bodies, the bylaws for the labour union representing financial workers has a specific section solely on negotiations, beginning with a subsection on authority stating that the Board of the Labour Union has the responsibility for and decision-making right in issues concerning negotiations. Prior to negotiations as to collective agreements concerning significant numbers of the members, the Board is to gather the viewpoints of the members and local clubs as well as call for a congress. The Board in this labour union is to continually keep the congress informed as to the negotiation proceedings and if deemed necessary, recall the congress. This section of the bylaws divides the negotiations into central and local negotiations, with the central handled by the Board or to a body delegated by the Board, and the local handled by the club within a company. The club is obligated to follow any guidelines as established by the union and submit any proposal to the union if such a procedure is established or if the proposed agreement can be deemed to affect the union's members in other banks and companies.

These bylaws state that a request for negotiations in certain issues can be presented by a concerned member or the union's local club. The request to negotiation is to be made by the Board or delegated body. An individual member, or group of members whose request for help in negotiations has been rejected, can bring an appeal to the Board.

The process as described starting with individual member suggestions, local club proposals, union proposals, all of which are addressed at the congresses, occurs both in the national labour unions and in the umbrella labour union organisations. Once the umbrella organisations determine their demands for collective agreements, the labour unions typically address these in some fashion. An example that can be given here is a press statement by the Paper Workers Labour Union last year, stating that the congress for the union had adopted the platform with respect to bargaining demands set out by LO, but that it also adopted a list with respect to the Union's own demands, including a specific wage increase, influence with respect to decisions concerning the use of temporary workers, security in employment with permanent employment, shortening of work hours, education in employment and greater equality in wages.

3.3. The internal dynamics of labour unions

A typical model for labour unions in Sweden is a three-level system, national and local, each having different tiers as follows:

Umbrella organization: Most belong to either LO, TCO or SACO,

National:

- Congresses (*kongresser*).
- The Board for the Labour Union (*förbundsstyrelse*).
- The Agreement Council or Representative Organ, and

Local:

- Divisions.
- Regional Groups.
- Local Clubs (*avdelningar*).
- Representatives at the workplace.

There can also be policy committees within a labour union, such as for students or retired persons. The major decisions as made by the labour unions are taken up at the congresses, and voted on by the representatives elected to the congress by the local clubs.

The decisions with respect to the local clubs are taken at the member meetings, and between such, by the board of the local unit. Annual meetings of the members are to be held, and every member has the right to take up an issue at the meeting (with a 14 day notice typically) and has one vote. The board of the local unit has several tasks as typically set out in the bylaws, including exercising the labour union's right of negotiation in local negotiations.

The Agreement Council or Representative Organ is an advisory committee to the Board for the Labour Union in questions that are deemed to be of greater principal significance. This Organ is also the deciding body with respect to issues concerning collective agreements. It has the task of accepting or rejecting proposals concern central collective agreements addressing wages and conditions of employment. It also takes the decisions with respect to industrial action. These rights can be delegated by the Organ to the Board of the Labour Union. With the Teachers' Union, for example, 119 representatives for the voting districts, appointed for one year, are the members in this organ.

The Board for the Labour Union is its executive body and acts on behalf of the Labour Union for the periods between the congresses. Its composition is set- out in the bylaws. For example, the board for the Teachers' Union has a chair, first vice chair and a second vice chair, and then 14 members as elected by the congress. Included in its duties is exercising the negotiation right of the labour union, accepting or rejecting central agreements on wages and employment conditions affecting less than three per cent of the union's members and accepting or rejecting central collective agreements within the framework of already adopted central collective agreements.

The congresses are the highest decision-making body in the labour unions, much akin to the shareholders in a corporation. A congress is held at certain intervals, often four years. For the Teachers' Union, there are 255 representatives, 251 from the voting districts, with mandates of four years, from congress to congress. Motions can be submitted to a congress by the local clubs, committees or individual members. A motion made by an individual member is to be brought seven months prior to the congress to the local unit. The local unit is to either issue its opinion as to the motion, or adopt the motion as its own. All motions are to be submitted to the Board of the Labour Union six months prior to the congress.

3.4. The bargaining system from the member perspective

The entire system with respect to bargaining demands, from beginning to the end of reaching a collective agreement, can be outlined as follows, at least for the blue-collar private sector:

Inputs are gain from several sources:

- The Congress.
- Views from members and representatives at work places.

- Motions from members.
- Within the sector, from the Economic Council discussed above under the 2011 Agreement, the Industry Council, and the Agreement Platform as formed within the sector.
- Inputs from the umbrella organisation, LO, from the LO Agreement Council, the Board of the LO, decisions by the Congress, and the Agreement Platform as formed within the LO.

These inputs are submitted to the Agreement Council, which typically functions as an advising body to the Board of the Union. These advisory bodies usually consist of representatives from each voting district, in large unions often over one hundred persons.

The Agreement Council submits a proposal to the board of the labour union. The board approves the proposal and submits it to the bargaining delegation. The bargaining delegation then submits the proposal to the employer/employer organisation by a certain date, upon which date the employer/employer organisation is to also submit its proposal. Negotiations then follow. Once an agreement is hammered out between the delegation and employer side, the delegation submits the proposal to the board of the labour union that in collaboration with the Agreement Council accepts or rejects the proposal.

Certain unions have a system where collective agreements affected members of the national employee organization other than those of the union signing have to go through some type of approval after the signing. Other unions, for example the Teacher's Union, have a system where proposed collective agreements with terms affecting more than 3% of the national organizations' members must be approved of by the central council (*Representantskapet*), which is the national organization's highest decisional body with respect to collective agreements. Contracts affected less can be approved by the Board of the union. The boards of the local clubs decide on the process for evaluating proposals. The decisions made by the central bodies in the unions are typically entered into the minutes of the body, attested to, and then deemed valid. The chair of the national union typically signs the agreements concerning wage and employment terms on the national level.

3.5. Information and education – effective representation

Two components are deemed necessary by the labour unions in order for them to provide effective representation, information and education. As stated above, the statutory primary right to negotiate includes an obligation for the employer to provide detailed information on the subject-matter of the negotiations, with several collective agreements not only providing access to documents, but also requiring the employer to pay for experts with whom the labour unions can confer in order to better understand the information provided as under the 1982 Efficiency Agreement.

As to the second component, education, the board for the local clubs often has among its duties as set out in the bylaws responsibility for the educational programs and operations for union activities on a local level. The board for the labour union can have the same duty on the national level. Generally, there seems to be the endeavour that everyone in the union, from the members up, is to work towards the union's goals, and to that end, have an understood duty to keep themselves up-to-date with respect to developments, policy, legislation, etc. The Teacher's Union can be used here again as an example, their Board has the specific duty to continually develop their competence and is to review this when adoption the annual operational plan. New board members are given an introduction course as to their duties, etc. In addition, each board member has the right to a mentor if they so wish.

Most of the labour unions also have periodicals that they publish and send to their members. The central umbrella organisations also attempt to reach members digitally, for example, LO has an app for i-phone and android that allows members to receive the latest news and video clips with respect to the collective agreement negotiations (*avtalsrörelse*), including podcasts.

The three umbrella organisations, LO, TCO and SACO, have courses given at community colleges (*folkhögskolor*), in three areas in Sweden, as well as an offering of Internet courses. The courses address issues for students, members, union representatives, negotiators and other persons having certain positions. All members have a right to a basic education with respect to unions. The objectives with the member education are to strengthen the awareness of members as to the unions, and encourage members to exercise their democratic rights in union organisations, at the work place and in society. A third reason given is to allow the union movement to continue to be a folk movement, necessitating members who participate in basic union courses and education. LO and certain unions have also set up scholarships to stimulate the creation of study groups. The Board of LO has stated that the focus on education for union members out to give knowledge as to the ideas that build the union promise: That wage earners promise each other to not sell their work at a lower price or at lower conditions than those which they have promised each other. The labour union is this promise. In addition, knowledge must be gained as to the most important means for this promise, the national collective agreements. Training and classes are often also available for union representatives, often given by the labour unions themselves, directed at representatives with tasks in the clubs, sections and divisions.

4. Information technology, social media and the unions

This system as described above is characterized by a high degree of self-regulation by the social partners (a bipartite system as opposed to tripartite system), based firmly on a consensus/democracy at the workplace discourse. Inputs by members can occur at many levels within the Union organization and during the collective bargaining process, making this system eminently suitable in some ways for the use of information technology and social media. This system has been challenged by both globalization and Europeanization in the form of freedom of movement of workers and services, as well as by the shift from collective rights to individual rights (based on Union law requirements). Another challenge to the system has been with respect to membership, with the Unions facing the need of reinventing themselves in order to follow the societal progression from an agricultural, to industrial, to services, and now the present information society. Social media and information technology can be seen as being invoked by the social partners in this pursuit of reinventing themselves, as well as with creating consensus with respect to the agreement demands.

All of the central social partners, on both the employer and employee sides, as a rule have a presence and use social media, facebook, twitter and RSS to reach out to their members and to a certain degree the general public. Youtube is used to capture certain events so that they can be disseminated further and over a longer period of time. One example that can be mentioned here is a blog with respect to the 2013 wage negotiations for doctors, entitled "Avtalsrörelsen 2013 fortbildning", preparing them for the pending collective bargaining negotiations. Blogs are also created for many union members to allow them to share their views. The umbrella labour union, Unionen, has on its editorial web page, unionenopinion.se (accessed 25.11.2013), a tab for social media. One of the more recent articles there was that a strike of ten employees in the town of Fränsta was supported by over 24 000 reactions in social media.

Publications as distributed by the social partners as referenced above are now also often available through technological means other than print. Just one example here is the member newsletter of the Swedish National Union of Construction Workers (www.Byggnadsarbetaren.se, accessed 25.11.2013) which as of June 2012 is available for smartphones with a like/dislike function. Other functions on the web include surveys with respect to specific questions, for example whether the unemployment forms are difficult to understand (June 2013). There is even a site containing links to twenty-one of the union publications in the blue collar sector, www.fackliganyheter.nu (accessed 25.11.2013). Teknikföretagen, an employer's organization, went totally digital with their newsletter beginning November 2012.

As discussed above, the education of union members is seen as a central task for the labour unions. In addition to classroom teaching, several unions have taken their traditional courses with respect to labour law and have made them available as on-line courses, allowing for a greater flexibility and participation by members. One example is SEKO's IT School, www.seko.se (accessed 25.11.2013). Another example is the public employee union ST's e-learning course with respect to wage development. With respect to employment law generally, there is one app called labour law, *Arbetsrätt* app which downloads pertinent to a smartphone. Another is *Ny som chef* (New as a boss), for new corporate managers, as well as one called Proud boss.

An example of the technology available to a union member can be seen with the Swedish Electricians Union (SEF). Members can download a calendar with all the important SEF dates, including the meeting dates for the Congress, submission dates, etc., as described above. Members can also download the webpage as adapted to smartphones at sef.se, as well as have a webpage dedicated to SEF-films, either on the Internet or as a web-app for a smartphone. The films cover diverse topics from the 2013 collective bargaining that is underway, as well as several from the 2012 collective bargaining negotiations. Other films concern ergonomic work, computer programs and legal assistance insurance coverage. A last app for SEF is Your Lawyer in Your Phone (*Din jurist i mobilen*), allowing members to send questions to lawyers as provided under the SEF insurance, as well as receiving answers via telephone.

Given the process of negotiation described above with respect to the internal workings of the social partners, as well as with respect to the collective bargaining between the social partners, the majority of the larger labour organizations has infused this process with technology. Some, such as Teknikföretagen, an employer's organization representing 3 500 employers, have their own apps for smartphones so that member can have all the news and negotiations sent directly to their telephones. Some such as SEF above have created news sites and films. The umbrella organization for municipal workers, Kommunalen, has a cite where members can sign up to receive an SMS with respect to the collective bargaining negotiations of any of approximately 20 different unions. Several unions have also had apps that allow the members to follow the negotiations as to the terms and conditions of the collective agreements and immediately signal a "like" or "dislike" as to the individual terms with respect to collective agreement.

The blue-collar umbrella organization LO as created a website for the 2013 collective bargaining negotiations, www.avtal13.nu (accessed 25.11.2013), where members of the affiliated national unions can access news articles, comment, place them on facebook, like, or twitter with respect to the content of the news articles. Videos with respect to the negotiations can be watched.

The negotiation demands can be downloaded, with several different individuals who can be twittered, along with a general twitter #avtal13. Questions can be sent by e-mail which answers are on the website. In essence, the entire negotiation process from its inception to the actual agreement can be followed and commented on by the members. According to Unionen, one of LO's national unions, over 1 000 individuals have twittered almost 7 000 times at #avtal13 as to the 2013 wage negotiations as of May 2013. The three most popular negotiation demands in the social media concern wages, parental leave pay and pensions. Unionen also listed the tweets received, with Unionen having received 1283, LO 898 and another union, IF Metall 587.

5. Conclusion: Enhanced or restricted?

A main effect of the Swedish model as outlined above is that those individuals who are not members of a union, or members of a more marginalized union, have had little to say with respect to the terms and conditions as agreed upon by the social partners. Outsiders in the historical context have been those persons who were not members of the union, and plausibly those not actively employed.

With the use of technology by the social partners as outlined above, the definition of outsiders arguably needs to be reassessed. A primary drawback of the use of information technology and social media within the system as created by the Swedish labour law model, is that it can be seen to increase the gap with respect to insiders and outsiders, union members and non-union members, while at the same time expanding the definition of outsiders in this context to other categories of persons who are union members. The first and most apparent category comprises those members who are not technically savvy. Another group that becomes more vulnerable with the use of technology in this context is those who are not proficient in the Swedish language. Such individuals are more vulnerable in a technologically based system as there is no human being who perhaps can explain issues in a different way or with a different language. Google translator, though an enticing exercise, is seldom accurate with respect to contracts and legal terminology on a large scale. A third group that becomes outsiders in this context are those individuals who cannot financially afford the equipment necessary to participate fully in the technology, thus in essence creating a divide based on socioeconomic grounds. According to one LO Report on digital participation,[21] 1.3 million Swedes of 9 million total, in other words, approximately 14% of the Swedish

[21] LO 2013 projekt: Digital delaktighet, for more information on this project in Swedish, see www.lo.se (accessed 25.11.2013).

population, never or seldom use the Internet. Of these, 400 000 are under the age of 60, and of these 61% are employed. This leads us to the fourth category of outsiders under the expanded definition, those who are older and have not be exposed to technology to the same extent as younger generations. Within this same project is the statement by LO: "For LO, the Internet is about freedom of choice and democracy. To be able to use the Internet is to be a full citizen. This is what we want everyone in Sweden to be".

The use of information technology and social by the Swedish social partners can be seen as a means to counteract the pressures that have been placed on the Swedish model, both politically and globally, in addition to the need to reinvent themselves to be more suitable for an information society. IT can be seen as a means for increasing democratic participation among the members of the social partners. At the same time, it can be seen as a means for exacerbating the gap between insiders and outsiders in the system, consequently decreasing democratic participation in a system in which the typical checks and balances of power do not exist due to its self-regulating nature. Under the system created by the Swedish labour law model, the social partners act not only as law-makers through collective agreements, but also enforce both the terms of the collective agreements and in some circumstances, even the adherence to statutory requirements. Given this heavy and significant role of the social partners, it is imperative that the channels of participation and democracy are broadened and not narrowed. Information technology and social media are a way forward in our information society, but it must be ensured that they are invoked as tools to increase and enhance democratic participation rather than of restricting it.

Chapter 8

Protection of the Consumer in Digital Content Contracts

Agnieszka Kubiak-Cyrul
Krakowska Akademia im. A.F. Modrzewskiego

1. Introduction

The digital revolution that has taken place over the past two decades with the gradual development of the Internet has profoundly altered the means of promoting and selling products and services offered by business entities. In these changed circumstances disputes concerning the situation relating to the use of the Internet by commercial companies are increasingly present. However, changes to the law cannot keep up with the pace of technological development. Consequently, the resolution of such disputes often requires the use of traditional legal concepts that were not originally designed for application to virtual reality. Such disputes may indeed raise questions about the meaning of such traditional legal concepts. One example which can illustrate this problem is related to consumer protection, well established in relation to contracts in the real world, but uncertain in virtual reality.

It is important to note that the consumer contract differs from other types of contracts.[1] Usually consumer contracts are pre-drafted by one party (professional trader), without the possibility of an amendment or re-negotiation of its content. Consumer contracts are usually executed between parties with unequal market power and knowledge. This is particularly true for B2C (business-to-consumer) digital content contracts. In order to protect the consu-

[1] For an overview of consumer law: E. Łętowska, *Europejskie prawo umów konsumenckich* (*EU Consumer Contract Law*), Warszawa 2004.

mer in B2C transactions, the separate body of law was created on the level of EU and subsequently in Member States legal systems. To ensure a high level of protection for consumers, EU consumer laws provides information duties for traders, formal requirements for contracts, right of withdrawal, remedies in case of non-conformity, protection against unfair contract terms or unfair commercial practices. The main objectives of EU legislation was to ensure informed consumer consent and to prevent any potential fraud or abuse of the consumer's weaker position, before the conclusion of, at the moment of, or during the performance of the contract. However, until recently, digital content products were not explicitly mentioned in EU legislation related to consumer contracts and no specific consumer protection rules pertaining to digital content services existed.

The EU acquis for consumer contracts contains a number of directives establishing minimum consumer protection requirements.[2] For the purposes of this paper, the most important EU consumer laws are: Directive 97/7/EC on the protection of consumers in respect of distance contracts (Distance Selling Directive),[3] Directive 1999/44/EC on certain aspects of the sale of consumer goods and associated guarantees (Consumer Sales Directive),[4] Council Directive 93/13/EEC on unfair terms in consumer contracts (Unfair Contract Terms Directive),[5] Directive 2005/29/EC concerning unfair business-to-consumer commercial practices in the internal market (Unfair Commercial Practices Directive).[6] As was already said, digital content products supplied online were not explicitly mentioned in this laws and there is serious controversy to what extent they are subject of the above mentioned provisions. Only Directive 2011/83/EU on consumer rights (Consumer Rights Directive CRD) contains provisions dealing expressly with digital content, but it is currently in the process of implementation by Member States and will be in force in June 2014.[7]

---

[2] For an overview of Consumer Law within the European Union, see: H. Schulte-Nölke (ed.), *EC Consumer Law Compendium, Comparative Analysis*, Bielfeld 2008, http://www.eu-consumer-law.org/consumerstudy_intro_en.pdf (accessed 01.11.2013).

[3] Directive 97/7/EC of the European Parliament and of the Council of 20 May 1997 on the protection of consumers in respect of distance contracts – OJ L 144, 4.6.1997, p. 19–27.

[4] Directive 1999/44/EC of the European Parliament and of the Council of 25 May 1999 on certain aspects of the sale of consumer goods and associated guarantees – OJ L 171, 7.7.1999, p. 12–16.

[5] Council Directive 93/13/EEC of 5 April 1993 on unfair terms in consumer contracts – OJ L 95, 21.4.1993, p. 29–34 Directive 2011/83/EU of the European Parliament and of the Council of 25 October 2011 on consumer rights – OJ L 304, 22.11.2011, p. 64–88.

[6] Directive 2005/29/EC of the European Parliament and of the Council of 11 May 2005 concerning unfair business-to-consumer commercial practices in the internal market – OJ L 149, 11.6.2005, p. 22–39.

[7] Directive 2011/83/EU of the European Parliament and of the Council of 25 October 2011 on consumer rights – OJ L 304, 22.11.2011, p. 64–88.

The goal of this paper is to discuss the legal status of the consumer in digital content contracts concluded and executed over the Internet in EU law. It seems that present regulations offer a lower level of consumer protection in digital content contracts than in the case of contracts for the acquisition of tangible goods. It is not surprising since EU consumer law began its life long before the Internet era and was not designed with the modern web in mind. EU consumer law was created for contracts related to tangible, movable goods. As a result, certain rules and remedies in consumer sales law are not compatible with the nature of the digital content and do not help to solve eventual consumer concerns regarding the accessibility, safety and functionality of digital content. If there are provisions in general contract law related to digital content contracts, they usually do not have a mandatory character. The redress mechanism provided by general contract law is too complicated for the average consumer. There is also little case law which interprets how the general contract framework applies to digital products. As a result, consumers and businesses find it difficult to identify and understand their legal rights and obligations in electronic commerce. Few consumers are willing to pursue their rights, when the benefits of doing so are so hard to predict without expensive legal advice.

2. Notion of digital content

For the purposes of this paper, digital content products are defined as products purchased via the Internet, delivered to the consumer online via streaming, downloads or as an access to the storage on the ICT platform, without a durable, physical, tangible medium. It includes computer programs, applications, navigation services, games, ringtones, photos, music, videos, e-books, etc. The advancement of Internet and mobile technologies has resulted in the constant enrichment and diversity of formats and access channels to digital content. Most consumers have access to the Internet through: computers, Internet enabled TV's, tablets, smartphones, e-book readers.[8]

The existing EU legal regime of consumer protection pre-dates the digital content era and does not provide any specific legal provisions in this scope. As a result, the first legal definition of digital content in the context of consumer protection appeared in the recent Consumer Rights Directive 83/2011. The lack of a common standard in this area causes serious inconsistency among the legal systems of EU Member States in how to regulate rights and

[8] OECD (2013), "Protecting and Empowering Consumers in the Purchase of Digital Content Products", OECD Digital Economy Papers, No. 219, OECD Publishing, http://dx.doi.org/10.1787/5k49czlc7wd3-en, p. 8 (accessed 01.11.2013).

obligation of parties in B2C digital content contracts. Usually, digital content products tend to be treated as 'goods' if they are provided in a physical format (on CD or DVD). However, where such products are delivered via 'intangible media', they fall outside of the conventional definition of 'goods' and outside the consumer protection offered for 'goods'. As a result, a consumer purchasing for example a music CD benefits from well-established rules of protection and a clear system of redress, while a consumer downloading the same music online, has problems with finding the legal basis for claims. This has left a significant gap in consumer protection.

There is also a tendency to think that if something is not 'goods', it must be a service. There has been much academic debate as to whether digital content is a good or a service.[9] This distinction is important as different legal consequences are attached to a consumer contract depending on whether the transaction relates to goods or services. In general, the service rights framework is based on the principle that the service should be provided with 'reasonable skill and care'. While the supplier of goods is strictly liable for the goods supplied, liability for the supplier of services is based on a negligence standard. The supplier of services is only liable if a breach of the duty of reasonable skill and care is proved. The ease of proof that the supplier was negligent is on consumer shoulders. In addition, if the reasonable care term is breached, the remedies available to the consumer are provided by general contract law and fall outside the consumer law. So applying the services framework to digital content could increase the existing legal uncertainty.[10]

At the same time, including digital content in the definition of 'goods' is also problematic. One of the reasons which have to be taken into account is the problem that digital content has with the subject of copyright. In a typical transaction of sale of goods, the title of ownership is passed to the consumer. In the case of a digital content contract, the supplier is not required to transfer the copyright pertaining to the digital content. Merely the right to use the digital content product is passed to consumer. However, the consumer can only use the digital content as set out in the license.[11] It is not clear to what extent the consumer may expect to be able to make a private copy or backup copies of digital content, or "resell" unwanted items. There is only one express

---

[9] 'Final report. Analysis of the applicable legal frameworks and suggestions for the contours of a model system of consumer protection in relation to digital content contracts'. University of Amsterdam research commissioned by the European Commission (2011), http://ec.europa.eu/justice/consumer-marketing/files/legal_report_final_30_august_2011.pdf (accessed 01.11.2013), p. 39. Further quoted as: University of Amsterdam. Final report 2011.

[10] Ibid., p. 172.

[11] See: R. Bradgate, *'Consumer Rights in Digital Products: A research report prepared for the UK Department for Business, Innovation and Skills'*, Sheffield 2010, http://www.bis.gov.uk/assets/biscore/consumer-issues/docs/c/10-1125-consumer-rights-in-digital-products (accessed 01.11.2013).

regulation of this problem in art. 5 of Computer Program Directive 2009/24/EC.[12] The lawful purchaser of a computer program has the rights to make a backup copy of the program, if this is necessary for its use, and in accordance with its purpose. This right may not be set aside by contract.

It is obvious that many digital content contracts also cover specific services related to digital content, such as delivery of digital content by download, access to game online, updates to digital content e.g. for antivirus or operating systems, streaming of digital content, access to software supplied in the cloud, storage of consumers own digital content in the cloud, upkeep to virtual worlds, etc.[13] Such related services can be defined as any service provided by the supplier of the digital content under the contract for the supply of digital content or a separate related service contract which was concluded at the same time. Related services, i.e. downloading or streaming processes, are often provided by the same digital content provider. It is also important to note that such services are essential to the delivery of digital content and are often so intertwined that a consumer's use of the digital content is dependent on the quality of the related service. It would be extremely difficult for a consumer to distinguish whether it was the digital content or the related service, which failed to comply with the quality standards.

There is also a proposition to overcome the distinction "goods or services" by developing a *sui generis* regime of tailored made provisions for digital content contracts where it is needed. Taking this approach, it is possible to apply an existing set of rules and adopt new or modernize the old ones, if it is necessary to, for the specific needs of digital content contracts.[14] Currently this opinion has prevailed and EU directive 83/2011 enacted provisions specifically tailored for digital content products supplied online.

---

[12] Directive 2009/24/EC of the European Parliament and of the Council of 23 April 2009 on the legal protection of computer programs. OJ L 111, 5.5.2009, p. 16–22.

[13] The European Commission's proposal for a Regulation of the European Parliament and of the Council on a Common European Sales Law (CESL) introduced in art. 2 (m) a definition of related services – *'related service' means any service related to goods or digital content, such as installation, maintenance, repair or any other processing, provided by the seller of the goods or the supplier of the digital content under the sales contract, the contract for the supply of digital content or a separate related service contract which was concluded at the same time as the sales contract or the contract for the supply of digital content*, http://eur-lex.europa.eu/lexuriserv/lexuriserv.do?uri=com:2011:0635:fin:en:pdf (accessed 01.11.2013).

[14] University of Amsterdam. Final report 2011, p. 178.

3. Digital Consumers Concerns

International surveys present the analyses of consumer status in digital content contracts and identify the problems that consumers are experiencing in this area.[15] The most important concerns are related to information provided by the supplier, quality of and access to digital content products. First of all, consumers have a significant problem with the lack of information, i.e. related to access and compatibility, complaints and redress mechanisms. Sometimes information provided by the supplier is difficult to find, or is unclear, or too complex. Information about the digital content product can be difficult to understand due to the length and manner of the presentation of the information, or the sophisticated language used. The importance of proper information cannot be overestimated, taking into account that the consumer is not able to inspect the digital content prior to purchase and is therefore particularly reliant on the description of the digital content product provided pre-contractually.[16]

Consumers also experience problems with the quality of digital content products, i.e. poor visual or sound quality, corrupt content, that could not function on the consumer's device, and sometimes caused damage to the device itself. It has to be underlined that in many cases there is no clear standard as to what a consumer can reasonably expect from a digital content product, what is 'normal' in digital content, which level of functionality consumers should be entitled to expect.[17]

Problems with access to digital content were also raised by consumers. Usually they had the form of unexpected service interruptions which could relate to Internet connection problems or be caused by issues with interoperability and technical protection measures in cases where consumers are only able to use digital content on certain devices. In addition, cross-border restrictions on digital content product use could cause problems for consumers.

---

[15] Instead of many: Digital products: EU consumers need clear rights – BEUC position paper. http://www.beuc.org/BEUCNoFrame/Docs/2/BEGAOPBAMAELDAGOIOLDNAJEPDWY9DBWAY9DW3571KM/BEUC/docs/DLS/2012-00832-01-E.pdf (accessed 01.11.2013). OECD (2013), "Protecting and Empowering Consumers in the Purchase of Digital Content Products", OECD Digital Economy Papers, No. 219, OECD Publishing, http://dx.doi.org/10.1787/5k49czlc7wd3-en (accessed 01.11.2013). N. Helberger, M.B.M. Loos, L. Guibault, Ch. Mak, L. Pesser, *Digital Content Contracts for Consumer*, Journal of Consumer Policy, 2013, No. 36, p. 37–57, http://link.springer.com/article/10.1007%2Fs10603-012-9201-1# (accessed 01.11.2013).

[16] Europe Economics, *Digital content services for consumers: Assessment of problems experienced by consumers*, http://ec.europa.eu/justice/newsroom/consumer-marketing/events/digital_conf_en.htm (accessed 01.11.2013).

[17] University of Amsterdam. Final Report, 2011, p. 25.

4. The regulatory framework in EU law

The relevant legal framework for digital content contracts encompass general contract law, consumer law and sector specific provisions, which can be found in particular in the field of intellectual property law, telecommunications law, audio-visual law, data protection law and e-commerce law. Taking into account the limits of this paper, only the following EU legislation will be presented: Directive on electronic commerce, Service Directive and some directives dedicated to protection of consumer – Distance Selling Directive and new Consumer Rights Directive.

4.1. Directive on electronic commerce

The background rules of general legal requirements for online contracting are provided in the Directive on electronic commerce (ECD).[18] It is the main legal act dealing with information society services. The ECD is designed to help remove obstacles to cross-border online services in the Internal Market. It regulates certain legal aspects of online services, i.e. certain information requirements, commercial communications, electronic contracting and the liability regime for online intermediaries. The term information society services is defined in the Directive 98/34/EC.[19] The definition of information society services covers any service normally provided, for remuneration, at a distance, by electronic means and at the individual request of a recipient of services. The concept of "at a distance" implies that the service is provided without the parties being simultaneously present. The expression "by electronic means" implies that the service must be conveyed from its point of departure to its point of arrival by means of electronic (processing and storage) equipment and by telecommunications means. Finally, the service must be provided via the transmission of data "at an individual request". This element of information society services sets them apart from other services that are sent without a request from the recipient being necessary.[20]

---

[18] Directive 2000/31/EC of the European Parliament and of the Council of 8 June 2000 on certain legal aspects of information society services, in particular electronic commerce, in the Internal Market ('Directive on electronic commerce') OJ L 178, 17.7.2000, p. 1–16.

[19] Directive 98/34/EC of the European Parliament and of the Council of 22 June 1998 laying down a procedure for the provision of information in the field of technical standards and regulations and of rules on Information Society services. OJ L 204, 21.7.1998, p. 37. For consolidated version: OJ 1.1.2013.

[20] Commission staff working document: Online services, including e-commerce, in the Single Market Brussels, 11.1.2012 SEC(2011) 1641 final; http://ec.europa.eu/internal_market/e-commerce/docs/communication2012/SEC2011_1641_en.pdf (accessed 01.11.2013).

Article 5 of Directive on electronic commerce requires the online trader to provide, as a minimum, the following information: name, geographical address, e-mail address, registration number, if registered in a trade, or similar public register. This information is important for consumers claiming their rights. In particular, the country of origin of the web trader can have major consequences for the scope of protection offered to the consumer. Article 5(1) of the ECD obliges also the online trader to establish an effective direct communication channel with its customers.

Articles 9–11 of the ECD contain essential and mandatory contracting requirements for online transactions. These conditions apply in addition to other EU requirements on contracts, such as pre-contractual information rights or unfair contract terms for consumer contracts provided in existing EU consumer *acquis*. The standard information requirements are listed in art. 10 of the ECD. On this basis, online traders must provide the consumer with specific information prior to the order being placed. This information should include in particular the steps to follow to conclude a contract, the filling of the contract by the service provider, the technical means for identifying and correcting input errors prior to the placing of the order, and the languages offered for the conclusion of the contract. In addition, online service providers must make any relevant codes of conduct, contract terms and general conditions easily available. Consumers should not only be able to store the contract terms and general conditions, but they must also be able to reproduce (print) them. The ECD also requires that in cases where the recipient of the service places her order through technological means, the trader has to acknowledge the receipt of the recipient's order without undue delay and by electronic means. The above mentioned obligations are often neglected.

4.2. Service Directive

Complementary provisions are provided by Service Directive 2006/123/EC.[21] The Services Directive aims at improving the regulatory environment for service providers who want to supply their services across borders to other Member States. Because of its general character, it is also relevant for online suppliers of digital content products. One of its goals is to strengthen the rights of recipients of services, which can be both consumers and businesses. For instance, it lays down a set of measures to promote a high quality of services and to enhance information and transparency relating to service providers and their services. A provider of the service is obliged to make available to recipients general information about service and assistance on

[21] Directive 2006/123/EC of the European Parliament and of the Council of 12 December 2006 on services in the internal market OJ L 376, 27.12.2006, p. 36–68.

the legal requirements, in particular consumer protection rules, and on redress procedures applicable in other Member States.

Article 22 of Service Directive contains the detailed information requirements which should be available to the service recipient. It encompasses in particular the following information: the name of the service provider, his legal status and form, the geographic address at which he is established and details enabling him to be contacted rapidly and communicated with directly and, as the case may be, by electronic means; where the provider is registered in a trade or other similar public register, the name of that register and the provider's registration number, or equivalent means of identification in that register; the general conditions and clauses, if any, used by the provider; the existence of contractual clauses, if any, used by the provider concerning the law applicable to the contract and/or the competent courts; the existence of an after-sales guarantee, if any, not imposed by law; the price of the service, where a price is pre-determined by the provider for a given type of service; the main features of the service, if not already apparent from the context. This information should be supplied by the provider on his own initiative or should be easily accessed by the recipient electronically by means of an address supplied by the provider. The time and transparency of this information is also regulated by the Service Directive. According to the art. 22(4) of Service Directive Member States shall ensure that the information which a provider must supply, is made available or communicated in a clear and unambiguous manner, and in good time before conclusion of the contract or, where there is no written contract, before the service is provided.

Since, in general, consumer service contracts are largely left unregulated in EU law, the universal legislation on services has to be applied. However, the scope of Service Directive is limited and major types of services are excluded.[22] Moreover, the Service Directive in principle does not affect the contractual relations between the service provider and the client, with one principal exception already mentioned – the information requirements imposed in art. 22 of the Services Directive. But even here it is important to noticed that certain information described in art. 22 of the Service Directive have to be provided without and others only upon request of the consumer.

4.3. Distance Selling Directive

Directive 1997/7/EC constitutes an important element in EU consumer contract law. It aims at ensuring that consumers who buy goods or services via distance selling means (for example Internet), without any face-to-face contact with the trader, are properly protected. The Directive covers both goods

[22] Art. 2 of the Service Directive.

and services. Article 4 of the Directive lists information the consumer must be supplied with, before entering into a distance contract. The Directive also prescribes the manner in which this information is to be given and its timing. According to art. 4 of Directive 1997/7, in good time prior to the conclusion of any distance contract, the consumer shall be provided with the following information: the identity of the supplier and, in the case of contracts requiring payment in advance, his address; the main characteristics of the goods or services; the price of the goods or services including all taxes; the arrangements for payment, delivery or performance; the existence of a right of withdrawal; where appropriate, the minimum duration of the contract in the case of contracts for the supply of products or services to be performed permanently or recurrently.

Moreover, Directive 1997/7 seeks to ensure the communication to the consumer of the information necessary to the proper performance of the contract. According to art. 5(1) of Directive 1997/7, the consumer must receive written confirmation or confirmation on another durable medium of the relevant information. According to EU Court of Justice, the terms 'receive' and 'given', used in that provision, refer to a process of transmission.[23] In a process of transmission of information, it is not necessary for the recipient of the information to take any particular action. In cases where the information found on the seller's website is made accessible only via a hyperlink sent to the consumer, that information is neither 'given' to that consumer, nor 'received' by him. As a result the requirements of the art. 5 (1) are not met when the relevant information is provided by the seller by sending to consumer a hyperlink to his website. It follows that a durable medium, within the meaning of art. 5(1) of Directive 1997/7, must ensure that the consumer, in a similar way to paper form, is in possession of the information referred to in that provision to enable him to exercise his rights where necessary. Only where a medium allows the consumer to store the information which has been addressed to him personally, ensures that its content is not altered and that the information is accessible for an adequate period, and gives consumers the possibility to reproduce it unchanged, that medium must be regarded as 'durable' within the meaning of that provision.[24] For digital content contracts, the information rules in the Distance Selling Directive are particularly relevant.

A consumer who buys goods or services at a distance is not able to fully assess the product when making the order, so the Directive provides consumer with a right of withdrawal of at least 7 working days (the so-called cool-

---

[23] See Case C-49/11. Judgment of the Court (Third Chamber) of 5 July 2012 (reference for a preliminary ruling from the Oberlandesgericht Wien – Austria) – Content Services Ltd v Bundesarbeitskammer. OJ C 145, 14.5.2011; http://curia.europa.eu/juris/document/document.jsf?text=hyperlink&docid=124744&pageIndex=0&doclang=EN&mode=req&dir=&occ=first&part=1&cid=2869120#ctx1 (accessed 01.11.2013).

[24] Ibid.

ing-off period). The common reason behind a right of withdrawal is to obtain time to rethink the conclusion of the contract. When the consumer exercises the right of withdrawal, all contractual obligations are extinguished. In exercising this right, the consumer does not have to justify this decision, must be refunded promptly and may only be charged for the cost of return. Under the Distance Selling Directive the cooling-off period for goods begins on delivery of the goods, but for services, the cooling-off period starts already at the moment when the contract is concluded. However, according to art. 6(3) of Directive 1997/7, the consumer may no longer withdraw from the contract, if she has given her consent for the performance of the service prior to the end of the cooling-off period. According to art. 6(3), there are other exemptions from the right of withdrawal. In particular it is related to the contracts for the supply of goods made to the consumer's specifications or clearly personalized or which, by reason of their nature, cannot be returned, for the supply of audio or video recordings or computer software which were unsealed by the consumer. On this basis Member States have a tendency to exclude or restrict the availability of the right of withdrawal for digital content contracts.[25]

4.4. Consumer Rights Directive

The new Consumer Rights Directive[26] (CRD) modernizes the existing highly fragmented consumer law. It covers the scope of the current Doorstep Selling,[27] and Distance Sales Directives, which will be repealed after Member States have transposed the new Directive. Laws to implement the CRD have to be adopted and published by the 13th December 2013 at the latest, and should apply from the 13th of June 2014. In general, CRD treats digital content products supplied on CD, DVD as a goods but it provide also tailored made provisions applying to digital content as its own category. It seems that the EU legislator, to some extent, is treating the supply of digital content as a sort of "quasi-sales contract". It can be justified by the "commodification" and standardization of digital content products through modern technologies.

Art. 2(11) of the Consumer Rights Directive provides that digital content means data which is produced and supplied in digital form. This definition is supplemented by the text in Recital 19 in the preamble:

---

[25] University of Amsterdam. Final Report, 2011, p. 81.

[26] Directive 2011/83/EU of the European Parliament and of the Council of 25 October 2011 on consumer rights, amending Council Directive 93/13/EEC and Directive 1999/44/EC of the European Parliament and of the Council and repealing Council Directive 85/577/EEC and Directive 97/7/EC of the European Parliament and of the Council Text with EEA relevance, OJ L 304, 22.11.2011, p. 64–88.

[27] Council Directive 85/577/EEC of 20 December 1985 to protect the consumer in respect of contracts negotiated away from business premises, OJ L 372, 31.12.1985, p. 0031–0033.

> Digital content means data which are produced and supplied in digital form, such as computer programs, applications, games, music, videos or texts, irrespective of whether they are accessed through downloading or streaming, from a tangible medium or through any other means. Contracts for the supply of digital content should fall within the scope of this Directive. If digital content is supplied on a tangible medium, such as a CD or a DVD, it should be considered as goods within the meaning of this Directive. Similarly to contracts for the supply of water, gas or electricity, where they are not put up for sale in a limited volume or set quantity, or of district heating, contracts for digital content which is not supplied on a tangible medium should be classified, for the purpose of this Directive, neither as sales contracts, nor as service contracts. For such contracts, the consumer should have a right of withdrawal unless he has consented to the beginning of the performance of the contract during the withdrawal period and has acknowledged that he will consequently lose the right to withdraw from the contract. In addition to the general information requirements, the trader should inform the consumer about the functionality and the relevant interoperability of digital content. The notion of functionality should refer to the ways in which digital content can be used, for instance for the tracking of consumer behaviour; it should also refer to the absence or presence of any technical restrictions, such as protection via Digital Rights Management or region coding. The notion of relevant interoperability is meant to describe the information regarding the standard hardware and software environment with which the digital content is compatible, for instance the operating system, the necessary version and certain hardware features.

The new Consumer Rights Directive improves and clarifies the information rights for consumers when purchasing digital content. In particular, traders will have to inform (consumer) buyers of digital content not only about its compatibility with hardware and software, but also about the application of any technical protection measures (TPM) or digital rights management (DRM), or other forms of limitation of access or use of digital content. It specifies how the right to withdraw applies to digital content in intangible and tangible form. However, the right of withdrawal is limited to situations where the performance of the contract has not yet begun or begun without the consumer's prior consent or, if the digital content is provided on a tangible medium such as a CD, where the consumer has not yet unsealed it. This means that consumers purchasing digital content can withdraw from the contract only before the downloading has started.

Unfortunately, CRD does not provide any specific rules which apply to defective digital products (e.g. a lack of functionality, inter-operability problems, poorer quality than expected, etc.). The existing system of legal guarantees and rules on conformity according to Consumer Sales Directive applies only to tangible goods. In the absence of tailored legal remedies, the consumer will have to seek recourse to the remedies that are available under general contract law.[28]

---

[28] University of Amsterdam. Final Report 2011, p. 124. M.B.M. Loos, Ch. Mak, *Remedies for buyers in case of contracts for the supply of digital content*. European Parliament's

5. Conclusions

One of the objectives in A Digital Agenda for Europe[29] was to establish a proper standard of protection for consumer in 'the digital age', because the lack of trust in the online environment was seriously hampering the development of Europe's online economy. The legal status of the consumer in digital content contracts was also the central theme in a number of academic researches. Thanks to the discussions following these publications, the legal status of the consumer in digital content contracts was partially improved. It was achieved via the Consumer Rights Directive by the introduction of specific rules on pre-contractual information, formal requirements related to conclusion of contract online and the right of withdrawal. However, there are still areas which need to be modernized or clarified, like the system of remedies in case of the nonconformity of a digital product with the contract.

Committee on Legal Affairs 2012, p. 7; http://www.europarl.europa.eu/document/activities/cont/201206/20120618ATT47122/20120618ATT47122EN.pdf (accessed 01.11.2013).

[29] Communication from the Commission to the European Parliament, the Council, the European Economic and Social Committee and the Committee of the Regions: A Digital Agenda for Europe COM(2010) 245 final/2, p. 13; http://eur-lex.europa.eu/LexUriServ/LexUriServ.do?uri=COM:2010:0245:FIN:EN:PDF (accessed 01.11.2013).

Chapter 9

Procedure, Time and Imputation in Criminal Law

Lorenz Schulz
Goethe University Frankfurt am Main

> "Actually I'm quite different. But I so rarely have time to show it" (Ödön von Horváth)[1]

1. Introduction

The body of contemporary criminal law falls into substantial and procedural criminal law. This division is relatively recent and not to be taken absolutely. Even in the German speaking tradition, where it is developed in a rather clear manner, there is a latent interplay between these branches, for the main procedural endeavour of gathering evidence is reflected in substantial law. If substantial law provides too many obstacles to gathering evidence, substantive norms are often eroded by interpretation or amended to ease evidence. In German law, where a substantive offence ("Tatbestand") is in general designed to secure a specific legal interest ("Rechtsgut"), one finds exceptions of criminal offences that are designed to secure the interest of getting evidence ("Ermittlungstatbestände"), most prominent in the offence of money laundering ("Geldwäsche", § 261 StGB).[2]

---

[1] "Eigentlich bin ich ganz anders, ich komme nur so selten dazu" (Ö. von Horvath, *Zur schönen Aussicht*, 1926). The German popsinger Udo Lindenberg adapted it in a song (together with Jan Delay, 2008) titled „Ganz anders". The refrain has Horvaths quotation ("Eigentlich bin ich ganz anders/ich komm' nur viel zu selten dazu/Du machst hier grad/mit einem Bekanntschaft/den ich ganz genauso wenig kenne wie du").

[2] In the same perspective, one finds the reduction of the elements of an offence, as in the offence of "Subventionsbetrug" (§ 264 StGB), by cutting some elements in the offence of fraud

Apart from the far-reaching division between substantive law and procedural law in the German speaking tradition, there are major legal systems where the division is not as strict. In a more procedural perspective, substantive matters are dealt with in a more pragmatic way. Thus, the separation of justification and excuse, a landmark in German criminal law, is less important in this perspective. This may be illustrated by the fact that the French and the Common Law doctrine has been so influential in International and European criminal law.[3]

Legal practitioners almost naturally defend a pragmatic approach. However, even in legal theory and in philosophy, pragmatism is mostly present in times of transition. In historical periods of transition, the maxim goes *res, non verba*. As in Latin *res* means legal affairs in the field of human action, this maxim is co-exentive with John Dewey's maxim *deeds, not creeds*. Since the Greek *pragma* is the word for action and the result of action, pragmatism is the proper term for this approach. Charles Peirce, the founder of American pragmatism, once noted that his famous pragmatic maxim means nothing more than the Biblical saying "You shall know them by their fruits" (Mark 7, 15).[4]

The development of the first internationally active banks took place in the 13th century, when the banking business started to flourish in Florence. However, the famous Medici's took the lead not because of the overly-prudent actions of their competitors but rather the role of the English king Edward III. It was his refusal in the 1340's to clear the huge debts he had run up in 1339 from the leading bank institutes of Florence Baldi and Peruzzi in order to finance the start of the Hundred Years' War the following year. Today, the Banca Monte dei Paschi di Siena, founded in 1472 as Monte di Pietà in Siena, claims to be the oldest bank in existence and is nowadays struggling as a result of its investment policy in the recent past.

In Siena, as well as in Florence, people will tell you that the Italian term *banco* or *banca*, the source of the term "bank", does not stem from the word

(§ 263 StGB) with the amendment of 1974, targeting a more effective prosecution of white collar crimes ("1. Gesetz zur Bekämpfung der Wirtschaftskriminalität"). A subtle way of reducing such an element is interpretation by the courts. A famous xample is the new interpretation of harm ("Schaden") in the offence of "Untreue" (§ 266 StGB). Irrespective of the economic advantages of using black money by companies, it is now a case of harm to merely establish a slush fund ("Schwarze Kasse") by providing money not listed in the balance sheet. Thus, the prosecution does not need to obtain evidence for specific offences of corruption (as in § 299 and §§ 332 ff StGB).

[3] J. Vogel, *Elemente der Straftat*, Goldtammers Archiv (GA) 1998, p. 127 ff; H.-H. Kühne, *Europäische Methodenvielfalt und nationale Umsetzung von Entscheidungen Europäischer Gerichte*, GA 2005, p. 195 ff.

[4] See L. Schulz, *By Their Fruits Ye Shall Know Them*, in: R. Kevelson (ed.), *Peirce and Law. Issues in Pragmatism, Legal Realism and Semiotics*, 1990, p. 131–151.

for desk but from taking a seat at the foot of the walls of many palazzos, where clients often had to wait for hours. Whatever the true story, it is a pity that modern bank buildings do not provide this convenient opportunity anymore for tourists to have a seat or to take a little nap.

The options business, the heart of modern finance capitalism, i.e. the risk activity seems to date back not only to the Italian Renaissance, but also to the earlier "Renaissance of the 12th century"; thus, in Italy, the Peruzzi's, the first finance capitalists, started to accumulate capital by trading with wheat grown in lower Italy, in exchange for textiles from Florence. The *ratio incertitudinis*, not the later Calvinist-puritan doubt about personal salvation, but that over the outcome of a merchants business, justified the exception that had to be made with respect to the Christian prohibition of taking interest rates. The purchase of the "aventure", the adventure, was the purchase of, for example, the expected catch of fishermen or the expected harvest of farmers, meaning literally the "in-come".[5] Whether the merchant, the business or mercantile man, operating internationally from his headquarters in a city like Florence, Siena, Venice or Augsburg in the case of the Fugger family, was already the most important social player after or next to the king,[6] may be somewhat doubtful, since the "engineer" had also been a powerful social figure since the 12th century, due to his importance in warfare as well as for the building of palaces and Gothic cathedrals.[7] In any case, from that time on we can detect specific aspects of a risk society, the systematic increase and dynamics of technical opportunities. Modern finance markets, trading with pure potentialities that we would call toxic, have a posteriori conquered the field of the possible that ratings agencies could not even measure anymore. The dynamics of a fully digitalized risk society has arisen from the acceleration or shortening of time up to the climax of simultaneity and ubiquity, i.e. omnipresence.

2. The conceptual frame

With respect to time as a category, we are used to speaking of objective and subjective time. The discovery of the later may be traced back to Augustine´s "Confessions" (Book 11) and anticipates modernity. The objectivity of time is reflected in Newton´s conception and, in philosophy, in Kant´s notion of

[5] M. Nerlich, *Abenteuer oder das verlorene Selbstverständnis der Moderne*, München 1997, p. 258–263.

[6] Ibid., p. 297.

[7] W. Krohn, *Die „Neue Wissenschaft" der Renaissance*, in: G. Böhme, W. von den Daele/ W. Krohners, *Experimentelle Philosophie. Ursprünge autonomer Wissenschaftsentwicklung*, Frankfurt/Main 1977, p. 3 ff, 65.

time and space as pure forms of apperception. This objective notion is altered by Einstein who relates time to gravity: The pilot who spends a lot of time in his cockpit becomes older than his fellow citizens on earth. Of course, he will not feel it because the difference consists only in fractions of a second over a period of a million years. In any case, Einstein´s observation was enough to slightly irritate our common sense. Naturally, we would like to have time (just like space) to be imaginable like a room without any furniture. This inclination leads to a debate between a Platonist and Aristotelian conception of time as not being settled yet,[8] although there are good arguments for the Aristotelian definition of time as measure of movement. In his essay *The Unreality of Time* (1908), McTaggart distinguished between two approaches (namely between a so-called A- and B-series). The A-series is characterized by concepts like "past", "present" and "prospective", relative to the ego-perspective of a speaker and, therefore, subjective to any other speaker. In opposition, the B-series has concepts like "earlier than" or "later than", related to other instances of time. Since the Earlier is always earlier than the Later, the B-series is independent from a subjective perspective. According to this scientistic conception of McTaggart, a conflict may arise between the A- and B-series. In that case, time would be illusory, which would at least be a consolation for the elderly.

At this point, I want to suggest a dichotomy of two modal principles in order to come to terms with our notion of time. Our common sense results from the Indo-Germanic structure of language based on the subject, or, in philosophical terms, on substance as a main category. Out of the ten categories Aristotle counted, one was substance and nine categories were related to substance. Movement, which is measured by time for Aristotle, is to be conceived of as rather fluid or dynamic. Nonetheless, it is limited by the teleological structure that Aristotle implants into every being (entelechy). The image of being is the possibility that is given in advance (dynamis) and designed to be actualized in the course of time, under good conditions (which, in the field of the *pragmata*, have to be provided by ethical behaviour).

The paradigm of the Hellenic concept of history is not the mythical notion of the eternal repetition of finite periods, but the notion of a linear, indefinite stream of time that is needed to actualize or realize the possibilities that are given, at least in principle, a priori.[9] This may be illustrated in law by the Aristotelian concept of the natural law. Contrary to the popular view, it is

[8] See F. Markosian, "*Time*", *The Stanford Encyclopedia of Philosophy* (November 2002; rev. February 2008, E.N. Zalta (ed.), *URL* = http://plato.stanford.edu/archives/win2003/entries/time/, sub 2; see sub 4 the references to John McTaggart Ellis McTaggart.

[9] See L. Schulz, *Das rechtliche Moment der pragmatischen Philosophie von Charles Peirce*, Ebelsbach 1988, p. 24 ff.

conceived as fluid, as a matter of change. The law of nature has "everywhere the same power (validity, dynamis)".[10] Reading the locus classicus, a relatively short section in the 5th book of the Nicomachean Ethics, Aristotle departs from the Sophist´s juxtaposition of the law of nature (physis), and positive law (nomos).[11] Then, we would expect the common illustration with Sophocles' *Antigone*, given in his Rhetoric, where natural law is eternal.[12] This, however, would confirm the Sophist´s objection to natural law conceptions as proposing something cut off from motion.[13] Without speaking of Antigone, Aristotle denies the objection by saying that, although the Gods may be motionless, nature is motion. This does not mean motion without structure. Thus, the content of the constitutions of the polis may be very different, but: "everywhere, there is one that is the best by nature".[14] Thus, with varying contents, we find as a structure the Socratic-Platonist structure of the best, that corresponds to the functional paradigm. That Aristotle does not give a more precise conception of his moderately conventional law of nature[15] may be due to his doctrine of the categories, where the laws of nature are neither a substance nor a contingent accident.

The modern notion of being is historically more indebted to the Jewish tradition than to the ancient Greek, as the prophets detected in their non-philosophical pattern of thought certain possibilities in God that had not been given before, not even in principle. Therefore, we may speak of "new" possibilities that were later specified by the apocalyptics. As a result of this discovery, time becomes increasingly important. Expecting the "eschaton", the realization of this possibility not given, the course of history becomes "fast" or "slow", "too late (in time)" or "just on time". Of course, these attributes also appear in the classic, Aristotelian model of possibility. But in the competing model this course of action is experienced as more of a drama, radicalized because of the consequences of imputing the results of action (pragmata) to acting subjects that are considered as important for the course of the action.[16] As soon as this expectation is connected to one´s action, as it is in Judaism because of the juridical framework of the covenant, expectation and responsibility are internally intertwined. *Impossibilium nulla obligatio est*: What is to be expected, is defined by the concept of the possible. Departing from the Attic concept of

---

[10] *Nikomachische Ethik*, Buch V, Kap. 10, 1134b 19¨C20.

[11] Ibid.

[12] *Rhetorics* I, 13, 1373 b.

[13] 1134b 24.

[14] 1135a 5.

[15] See H. Ottmann, *Geschichte des politischen Denkens*, Die Griechen, Tübingen 2001, No. 1/2, p. 152–154.

[16] This kind of determination presupposes the comparison of motions; see Augustine, *Confessions* XI, p. 20 ff.

history as the realization of given possibilities, this can then be accelerated. However, this accelerated history remains the history that was given ahead in principle.[17] Acceleration remains a "teleological" one.[18] This cannot be true of the *eschaton* in the competing model. Here, the actor is aware of being in a provisional state of being that is deemed to come to an end. History here is a discontinuous, dramatic development. The essential part of the drama is slowing down and accelerating. The experience of acceleration rests on the concept of a *kairos* as a critical moment, which mirrors that. In antiquity one has to detect this *kairos* to somehow manage the structurally given chain of being. With the competing model, a crisis may be patiently tolerated or may be improved as one gives Yahweh a hand.

The task of the Scholastics was to provide a synthesis of revelation and Greek tradition, resting on Platonism on the one hand, and, after his "baptism" by Aquinas, Aristotle on the other. This endeavour is entangled with the financial market as well as with a revolution of law focusing on the subjective rights of the actor (in general as, of course, in particular in the realm of the market). The chief witness of the synthesis of the paradigm of the possible and the dignity of the agent is Pico della Mirandola, who was favoured by the Medici's in Florence. His heretical speech, later called the *Treatise on Human Dignity* (1496), starts with: "Nothing can be more admired than man". Because of the imago Dei-nature of the human being, man is a micro-cosmos of possibilities of which he is the master.[19] Pico starts with the possible proceeding to being. This will be followed by equipping the subject of action, the actor, with the rights to secure the realization of the possible.[20] In the Scholastic tradition, the Franciscan Duns Scotus had already emancipated the possible from being by proclaiming the realm of the logically possible. The dynamics of this emancipation liberates the essential from being (*esse*) and gives the *actus essendi* a prominent role[21] that will be combined with subjective rights as kind of *ens quo* filling life into the empty shell of potentiality.[22] Departing

---

[17] R. Koselleck, *Der Traum der Vernunft. Vom Elend der Aufklärung*, Berlin 1985, p. 90.

[18] Ibid., p. 92, takes a different wording: for the first, he speaks of „acceleration" (Beschleunigung), for the second, of the "teleological concept of shortening time" (teleologischer Begriff der Zeitverkürzung).

[19] P. della Mirandola, *Über die Würde des Menschen/Oratio de hominis dignitate*, Hamburg 1990; for the importance of Pico see R. Gröschner, *Freiheit und Ordnung in der Republik des Grundgesetzes*, Juristenzeitung (JZ) 1996, p. 639; S. Kirste, *Einführung in die Rechtsphilosophie*, Darmstadt 2010, p. 127.

[20] See L. Schulz, *Subjektive Rechte und die Ausdifferenzierung von Kompetenz. Anfänge moderner Rechtsstaatlichkeit im Mittelalter*, in: *Subjekt und Kulturalität II: Zur Kulturalität von Scham, Schuld und Verantwortung*, ed. K. Seelmann et al., Berlin 2010, p. 229–248.

[21] See L. Schulz, *Normiertes Vertrauen*, Frankfurt/Main 2001, A II 1 b.

[22] See K.W. Nörr, *Zur Frage des subjektiven Rechts in der mittelalterlichen Rechtswissenschaft*, in: *Festschrift für Heinrich Lange*, ed. D. Medicus u.a., Stuttgart 1992, p. 200.

from these dynamics, the self-made man gains principal respect, as he economically realizes the possible. As a vehicle of the *actus essendi,* he becomes the pragmatic, sometimes even speculative manager of facticity.[23] Looking at the Franciscan tradition up to Ockham, this is combined with voluntarism. Authority will replaces rationalist truth: *non veritas sed auctoritas facit legem.*

3. Acceleration

Where money is tight, time is tight. Even our free time or leisure is subordinated to the paradoxical economy of time: the more we try to save time, the less we have of it. Even if we observe the "discovery of slow time" or the "ecology of time", speed has more friends. For Virilio, who treated acceleration almost obsessively,[24] speed and acceleration are the essential characteristic of modernity. Speed is the "last postindustrial source of income", that will consume its children as every revolution does. The "dromocratic" government, associated, with a "elite of movement", is contrasted by Virilio with a "democratic" speed, securing politics in combination with time. Of course, Virilio may merit the reproach of deconstructivism and apocalyptic thought (dividing history essentially into two eras). In any case, he shows sensibility for the radical dynamics of time.

The experience of acceleration is not peculiar to modernity. We may go back to the beginnings of modern industrialization.[25] Shortly after that, we can observe literary and scientific reflection on acceleration. New England´s historian Henry Adams analyzed the change of the Gilded Age, suggesting a "law of acceleration". According to this law, the accelerated future shortens the recourse to the past. Accordingly, history is reduced to examples that action does not provide guidelines for future actions anymore.[26]

This "saddle-time" (Koselleck), as a point of departure for modern history, leads to an orientation focusing on concepts of motion such as progress and regress, acceleration and hesitation. History as the history of acceleration is a concept that is at hand. Nature, therefore, would be opposed to the hubris connected with manmade acceleration. However, the idea that nature is indebted to slowness, is a misconception, as research on chaos structures shows.

---

[23] This explains the later nominalist-voluntarist criticism of the Scotistic conception.

[24] See P. Virilio, *Krieg und Kino. Logistik der Wahrnehmung*, Frankfurt/Main 1986; *Der negative Horizont. Bewegung/Geschwindigkeit/Beschleunigung*, Frankfurt/Main 1989; *Rasender Stillstand*, Frankfurt/Main 1992.

[25] See R. Koselleck, ibid.

[26] H. Adams, *The Education of Henry Adams*, New York 1931 (1918), p. 489 ff.

At the heart of the experience of this acceleration, as Koselleck points out, is the technical and scientific progress of that era.[27] However, because of the experience of crisis, the acceleration still is tangible in the language of the prophets. Did we not ever think that is five minutes to twelve? That the reference to such symbols is problematic is illustrated by the diagnosis of the present by H. Hofmann and Stratenwerth. For them, law´s function is to stop acceleration ("Aufhalter der Beschleunigung").[28]

4. Time and imputation in legal ethics and law

The leading German encyclopaedia of philosophy, the *Historisches Wörterbuch der Philosophie* (edited by J. Ritter, K. Gründer and G. Gabriel), was finally completed after three decades in 2007 and has been available since then for systematic research. This is helpful for the concept of time. Of course, there is time in philosophical, psychological, historical and literary respects. However, we do not detect it with respect to jurisprudence or social sciences, in political philosophy or sociology. Instead, we find it in the realm of theology and in the philosophy of history. Thus, the reflection on time with respect to imputation is certainly not easy.

This is remarkable because the potential for harm resulting from acceleration is immense. This is shown by the crisis of the financial markets, which has caused many attempts at regulation after many years of de-regulation. For the humanities that are concerned with legal issues, there are two important books which are internationally influential: Niklas Luhmann's *Law as a Social System* (2004, originally: *Das Recht der Gesellschaft*, 1993), and *Between Facts and Norms* by Jürgen Habermas (1992, originally: *Faktizität und Geltung*, 1992). The cipher of time in Habermas is the "risk of dissent".[29] As surprising contingencies are permanently nourishing this risk, social integration through language would be unlikely without the anchoring in deliberate communicative action, in the lifeworld (Lebenswelt), that is like a deeply seeded rock of consented patterns of interpretation, loyalties and capacities.[30] This heritage is jeopardized by the acceleration of the lifeworld and, therefore, needs to be reproduced by communicative action. Although the contingency reveals that value-orientated or anthropological concepts cannot be funda-

[27] "In der Praxis freilich färben sich beide Begriffe der Beschleunigung, der Erfahrungsbegriff und der Erwartungsbegriff, gegenseitig ein. Es kommt nur darauf an, sie analytisch zu trennen, um die utopischen Hoffnungen, die sich an die Beschleunigung geknüpft haben, nicht auf eine gefährliche Weise ausufern zu lassen". Ibid., p. 99. Experience (Erfahrung) for Koselleck means presented past, whereas expectation (Erwartung) stands for presented future.

[28] H. Hofmann, *Natur und Naturschultz im Spiegel des Verfassungsrechts*, JZ 1988, p. 278.

[29] J. Habermas, *Faktizität und Geltung*, Frakfurt/Main 1992, p. 37 ff.

[30] Ibid., p. 38.

mental, the tie of communicative action to the lifeworld is a heavy burden for that action, and thus time is tamed by the discourse of language. Habermas' idealization of this discourse, which makes universal claims in morals and law possible, is criticized for not taking tradition seriously and for dreaming of the successive abolition of time. Nonetheless, time is real in Habermas in the realm of legislation, where he situates the integration of society, instead of taking jurisdiction and its traditional nature as Luhmann does it.

In that respect, we can observe a complex typology of pragmatic, ethical and moral types of discourse and their integration within the process of legislation.[31] The communicative understanding of the three powers of the classic triad of power suggests an advanced conception of the doctrine of the balance of power. Thus, Teubner could read "Between Facts and Norms" as related to system theory, for he interprets it as a model to safeguard the collision of discourses that are equally original in nature.[32]

In Luhmann´s autopoetic systems theory, time is pervasive. Systems are defined by operations, by communication focusing on the code that is constitutive of system. This communication works out as long as it is connectable ("anschlussfähig"). Time in communication is located within expectation ("Erwartung").[33] The task of social integration has a dimension of time which is accomplished by stabilizing expectations. Precisely, this is the function of norms.[34] In the system of law as defined by the code of lawful and unlawful, connectability is safeguarded not by the legislator, but by the judicial system that is located at the heart of the system.[35] The imminence of time is constitutive. At the same time, it is subject to a paradoxical logic: decisions only come about in cases of fundamental indecision. Time is predominant:[36] the temporalisation of complexity leads to a rational increase in possibilities, i.e. to increasing discretion.[37] Operative systems produce the time they operate in and with.[38] Time is essentially relative to systems, it is not an element of the world, but a result of systematic operations.[39]

---

[31] Ibid., p. 197 ff.

[32] G. Teubner, Frankfurter Rundschau, 11.11.1992, p. 87.

[33] N. Luhmann, *Das Recht der Gesellschaft*, Frankfurt/Main 1993, p. 124 ff.

[34] Ibid., p. 134.

[35] Ibid., p. 7. Kap., p. 317.

[36] Ibid., p. 562.

[37] "Zieht man die Zeitdimension in Betracht, kommen die Vorteile der Temporalisierung von Komplexität in den Blick und Rationalität ließe sich dann begreifen als Vermehrung der einschränkbaren Möglichkeiten, als Vergrößerung des Entscheidungsspielraums mit Vermehrung der zeitabhängigen Entscheidungsbeschränkungen", ibid., p. 564.

[38] See A. Nassehi, *Die Zeit der Gesellschaft. Auf dem Wege zu einer soziologischen Theorie der Zeit*, Frankfurt/Main 1993, p. 3. Kap. ("Autoontologie").

[39] "Diesem systemrelativen Charakter der differenzierten Moderne entspricht ein strikt systemrelativer Zeitbegriff, der als intersystemische Zeitstruktur keine reale Zeit ansetzt, sondern wiederum nur die Systemzeit der Gesamtgesellschaft", ibid., p. 539.

For the German discussion on time and imputation in legal ethics and constitutional law, Stephan Kirste has given a helpful overview.[40] Departing from the conception of human dignity in Pico that focuses on the possibilities of man,[41] he deduces from this the right to have possibilities. In this way, he defines some objective and subjective means to safeguard a "justice of time" ("Zeitgerechtigkeit").[42] Within respect to criminal law, there is the right to hope for rehabilitation that is violated by lifelong incapacitation.

5. Time in substantive criminal law

Criminal law is the seismograph of imputation in law because it is concerned with the harshest infringement of the freedom of the individual.[43] It is not very common to focus on time in this context since at first sight one may not expect fruitful insights from treating with such a highly abstract topic.

The proper spot to treat the effects of acceleration in criminal law is the offence or *actus reus* (in German: "Tatbestand"; in French: "infraction"). According to the German doctrine that has influenced countries like Poland or Spain, but is not received in the Common Law tradition or in France, we have to look at the principles of objective imputation.[44] However, above all, this seems to imply too much philosophy. In German doctrine, the famous battle with Hans Welzel, the most important proponent of the finalist doctrine of action, resulted in a retreat from ontology. Thus, the examination of action as criterion of the *actus reus* has the plain function of eliminating some actions where the actor is not the master of his deeds.[45] Basically, this approach is to be followed even from a philosophical angle as in philosophy the recourse to an Aristotelian view on action is considered somewhat naive. If one does not want to treat acceleration in terms of agency, the criterion of harm ("Schaden", "Erfolg") comes next. Here, time is reflected in actions that lead to harm much later on. It is an action that, as you phrase it in German, "zeitigt Folgen". Then, you get to the locus classicus of time in law, limitation or prescription. This may be illustrated by a case of product liability in criminal law,

---

[40] S. Kirste, *Zeit und Rechtsethik*, in: *Rechtsethik*, hrsg. v. M. Fischer, M. Strasser, 2007, p. 93. For a brief introduction see L. Schulz, *Time and Imputation*, in: *The Philosophy of Law: An Encyclopedia*, ed. Chr.B. Gray, Shrewsbury 1999.

[41] Ibid., p. 103 f.

[42] Ibid., p. 107 ff.

[43] This is shown by detention that is a sacrifice for the business of prosecution that is indispensable for the state.

[44] Although we could treat it already by means of the concept of action ("Handlung").

[45] C. Roxin, *Strafrecht. Allgemeiner Teil I*, 4. Aufl., München 2004, § 8/32 ff.

the case of using wood preservatives.[46] This use in the 1970's and 1980's led to many symptoms that may be connected to a syndrome ("Holzschutzmittel-syndrom"). If one follows the analysis by a Frankfurt court, this syndrome is characterized by the effects of summation and long-time consequences that are again influenced by acceleration.[47] The indicted violation or infraction of bodily integrity does not show the syndrome, because one can live safely with it in a different environment.[48] If this diagnosis is correct, we have no absolute limitation anymore but a limitation that depends on societal needs, designated by the catchword of the exhaustion of the wrong ("Erschöpfung des Tatunrechts").[49] This contradicts legal certainty that is the target of limitation. Thus, we need a conception of limitation that safeguards non-utilitarian imputation ("beyond functionalism"/"jenseits des Funktionalismus").

The examination of the causal chain between harm and action is not of central importance from the point of view of the German doctrine, which defines causality as condition *sine qua non*. If action accelerates the effect only slightly, according to this point of departure, we have causality. The German high court, at least, presupposes a "relevant" acceleration.

Although the doctrine of objective imputation is relatively young and therefore still needs to be developed substantially, it leads into the right direction, i.e. contributes to reducing the wide field that was opened up by a rudimentary concept of causality in the sense of a condition *sine qua non* by the introduction of a requirement of setting and realizing a risk. This doctrine presupposes the model principle we have called the classical one: we can only impute possibilities that are given in principle. Of course, in some cases this is not easy to be determined. So-called secondary harms or effect harms result in problems that have not been solved.

Even within the limits of the classical principle, the thesis that time is irrelevant is doubtful in cases where effect harms are very late harms. One may concentrate on the "process of becoming historical", as some have suggested in HIV-cases.[50] This cannot be pursued here. More famous is the procedural

---

[46] LG Frankfurt, 25.5.1993, 5/26 Kls 65 Js 8793/84 ("Holzschutzmittel"), in part published in Zeitschrift für Umweltrecht (ZUR), 1994, p. 33.

[47] LG Frankfurt, ibid. (unpublished), p. 76 ff, 181 ff.

[48] "Bei der Zufügung chronischer Krankheitszustände stellt sich das Bild anders dar als nach einem Tritt oder Messerstich. Zwar ist die Tat vollendet, wenn der erste auf sie rückführbare Anfall oder Zustand beobachtet worden ist. Die Beendigung tritt aber erst Jahre später ein, wenn etwa der durch die immerwährende Diffusion biozider Inhaltsstoffe hervorgerufene Schaden nicht mehr abgewendet und nicht mehr vergrößert werden kann... Solange noch mit Aussicht auf gesundheitliche Besserung eingegriffen werden kann, ist die Handlung nicht beendet und beginnt die Verjährung nicht zu laufen". LG Frankfurt, ZUR, 1994, p. 38.

[49] L. Schulz, ZUR, 1994, p. 28.

[50] H. Schlehofer, *Risikovorsatz und zeitliche Reichweite der Zurechnung beim ungeschützten Geschlechtsverkehr des HIV-Infizierten*, Neue Juristische Wochenschrift (NJW) 1989, p. 2017, 2025.

side of the "distant effects" in the case of illegal measurements of prosecution. There, we also have to rely on the classic modal principle.[51] Finally, time and acceleration of time is important for the definition of the imputation figure of the "legal risk" ("erlaubtes Risiko"), that lies at the heart of the doctrine of risk society. Of course, the permission to act on risk is part of the law from the beginning of doctrine onwards. Modern society, however, has made this specific doctrine central to imputation.

In the subjective, mental element of imputation ("mens rea"; "élément moral") that is according to the modern framework located within the constitutive elements of a crime in the *actus reus* ("Tatbestand", "infraction"), it is the examination of the intention ("Vorsatz", "dol"), where acceleration has to be treated. Especially in white-collar crime, namely in the fiscal area, we can observe an inclination to get rid of the image of intention as a place where in criminal law, the state gives priority to ordinary ignorance, even to stupidity. Instead, we get more and more obligations to examine a situation, to inform us about risks.[52] To be clear about that: it is information not on the normative, regulative side that is treated as ignorance of law, but on the factual side. In German doctrine, Lothar Kuhlen has given a time-based conception for this kind of error or ignorance.[53] He departs from the consideration that *vis-à-vis* the temporalisation resulting in complexity and unclearness the actor has to be relieved of his burden.[54] Overcoming the traditional dichotomy of error of fact and error of law (in the German code: §§ 16, 17 StGB), he regards it as central to ask whether the *actus reus* is related in a static way to the primary criminal offences (Kernstrafrecht), or dynamically to regulations that are valid in the very moment of action ("zum jeweiligen Handlungszeitpunkt gelten"). As a result, it is the criterion of time that is decisive, not the sophisticated typology of elements of the definition of a crime as descriptive, normative, or accessory elements (Blankettverweisungen). Thus, this criterion of time[55] shows a principal de-substantialisation,[56] denying the classical model in favour of an open model. This may be justified as it does not conflict with the basic principle of the determinacy of a norm (principle of legality, Art. 103 II GG). There is no infliction because the openness favours the actor. Of course, one has to question the criterion of its practicality. Kuhlen´s argu-

---

[51] E. Kelnhofer, *Hypothetische Ermittlungsverläufe im System der Beweisverbote*, Berlin 1994.

[52] See F. Bielefeld, *Strafrechtliche Risiken der Steuerberatung*, Festschrift für Imme Roxin, Heidelberg 2012.

[53] L. Kuhlen, *Die Unterscheidung von vorsatzausschließendem und nichtvorsatzausschließendem Irrtum*, Frankfurt/Main 1987.

[54] Ibid., p. 398 ff.

[55] Ibid., p. 370 ff.

[56] Ibid., p. 400.

mentation suggests that, for him, it is the dichotomy of primary and accessory criminal law (Kern-/Nebenstrafrecht), which is the point of departure.

Beyond the mentioned problems of imputation on the surface of *actus reus* and *mens rea*, it is worth considering the effects that time and acceleration have for the principles of criminal law. Most important among them is the principle of legality, the mentioned requirement of determinacy (*nullum crimen, nulla poena sine lege*, Art. 103 Abs. 2 GG, with respect to the *lex certa*). The framework for an answer is defined by a development that may be illustrated by its conceptualization by Luhmann. He originally identified legal rules with conditional programs. Later, he modified his notion of law to include the distinction between conditional and teleological, purposive programs ("Konditional-" vs. "Finalprogramme"). The strict requirement of the *lex certa* requires conditional programs. For Luhmann, modernity means that primary, conditional legal regulations are replaced by secondary norms, which are present especially in administrative law,[57] connected with "co-operative" and "consensual" legislation.[58] Even more than in a discourse-theoretical perspective, in systems theory focusing on the evolutionary aspect, Teubner reflects that in his notion of a constitution beyond the state.[59] Where classical conditional programs are still prevalent in substantial law, one observes a more flexible procedural law enabling parties to negotiate the boundaries of the *lex certa*. The German legislator, e.g., has recently amended the procedural code in a section on "Verständigung" (§ 257c StPO), which the constitutional court has more recently agreed with.[60]

Reflecting on this development, one might be tempted to abolish the *lex certa* requirement entirely in favour of the open modal principle. However, this would be throwing the baby out with the bath water. The German constitutional court recently suggested a solution where legislation and jurisdiction co-operate in the endeavour to make criminal law regulations sufficiently determinate, while still adhering to the classical model principle.[61] The courts

---

[57] Cf. W. Hoffmann-Riem, E. Schmidt-Aßmann, A. Voßkuhle (eds*), Grundlagen des Verwaltungsrechts*, Band I, München 2006, p. 1085 ff.

[58] F. Becker, *Kooperative und konsensuale Strukturen in der Normsetzung*, Tübingen 2005.

[59] G. Teubner, *Constitutional Fragments: Societal Constitutionalism in the Globalization*, Oxford 2012 (German: *Verfassungsfragmente: Gesellschaftlicher Konstitutionalismus in der Globalisierung*, Berlin 2012; see also T. Vesting, *Rechtstheorie*, Darmstadt 2007. For the kmanifoldness of the transnational approaches in legal theory see S. Buckel, R. Christensen, A. Fischer-Lescano (ed.), *Neue Theorien des Rechts*, Stuttgart 2009, p. 345 ff (on "transnationalen Rechtspluralismus").

[60] BVerfG, 19.3.2013 (2 BvR 2628/10 etc.); see F. Stuckenberg, Zeitschrift für Internacionale Strafrechtsdogmatik (ZIS), 2013, p. 212 ff.

[61] BVerfGE 23. Juni 2010. See L. Schulz, *Neues zum Bestimmtheitsgrundsatz ¨C Zur Entscheidung des BVerfG vom 23. Juni 2010*, in: *Strafrecht als Scientia Universalis. Festschrift für Klaus Roxin zum 80. Geburtstag*, ed. M. Heinrich, Chr. Jäger, 2011, 305¨C331.

are obliged to eliminate remaining inclarity in applying a rule by specification through interpretation as much, as possible.[62] Most essential is that this determination is presented as the possibly best determination according to the principle of optimizing law ("Optimierungsgebot"). In effect, a change of legal interpretation in jurisdiction is subject to the *lex stricta* requirements, i.e. the prohibition of retrospective legislation (*lex praevia* requirement). The crucial aspect of this conception, the delegation of the power of defining crimes from the legislator to the court, is justifiable according to the German concept of separation of powers because the constitutional court monitors the courts and secures the safeguarding of the *lex certa* requirement, whereby the intensity of control depends on the seriousness of criminal sanctions.

6. Time in criminal procedure

The *loci classici* of time in law are: deadline ("Frist"), limitation ("Verjährung"), legal force ("Rechtskraft"), and, even literally close, the maxim or commandment of process acceleration. This maxim is considered to be a constitutional maxim resulting from fair trial (Art. 6/1 ECHR, Art. 20/3 and Art. 1/1, 2/1 German Basic Law). At first sight, this safeguards the subjective rights of the indicted. This is the fundamental notion of the European Court of Justice in Strasbourg, basically reflecting subjective rights in the bi-polar relation between the individual suspect and the prosecution by the state. As soon as we introduce a tri- or multipolar relation inducing the victim of a crime, we have to reflect this even with the maxim of acceleration. This is what the German constitutional court is now doing. For the constitutional court, accelerations also serve the needs of criminal procedure in view of what the victim desires. This leads in principle to an infringement of the rights of the suspect in favour of the economy of prosecution based on the inquisitorial principle to detect truth.[63] This manifold approach requires the safeguarding, in due course, of a time-based conception of investigation, where suspicion is dependent on effective prosecution.[64]

---

[62] "Verbleibende Unklarheiten über den Anwendungsbereich einer Norm durch Präzisierung und Konkretisierung im Wege der Auslegung nach Möglichkeit auszuräumen (Präzisierungsgebot)".

[63] L. Schulz, *Normiertes Misstrauen*, Frankfurt/Main 2001, I.

[64] Ibid., p. III.

Technical editor
Dorota Węgierska

Proofreader
Agnieszka Toczko-Rak

Typesetter
Hanna Wiechecka

Jagiellonian University Press
Editorial Office: Michałowskiego St. 9/2, 31-126 Kraków
Phone: 12 663 23 81, 12 663 23 82, Fax: 12 663 23 83